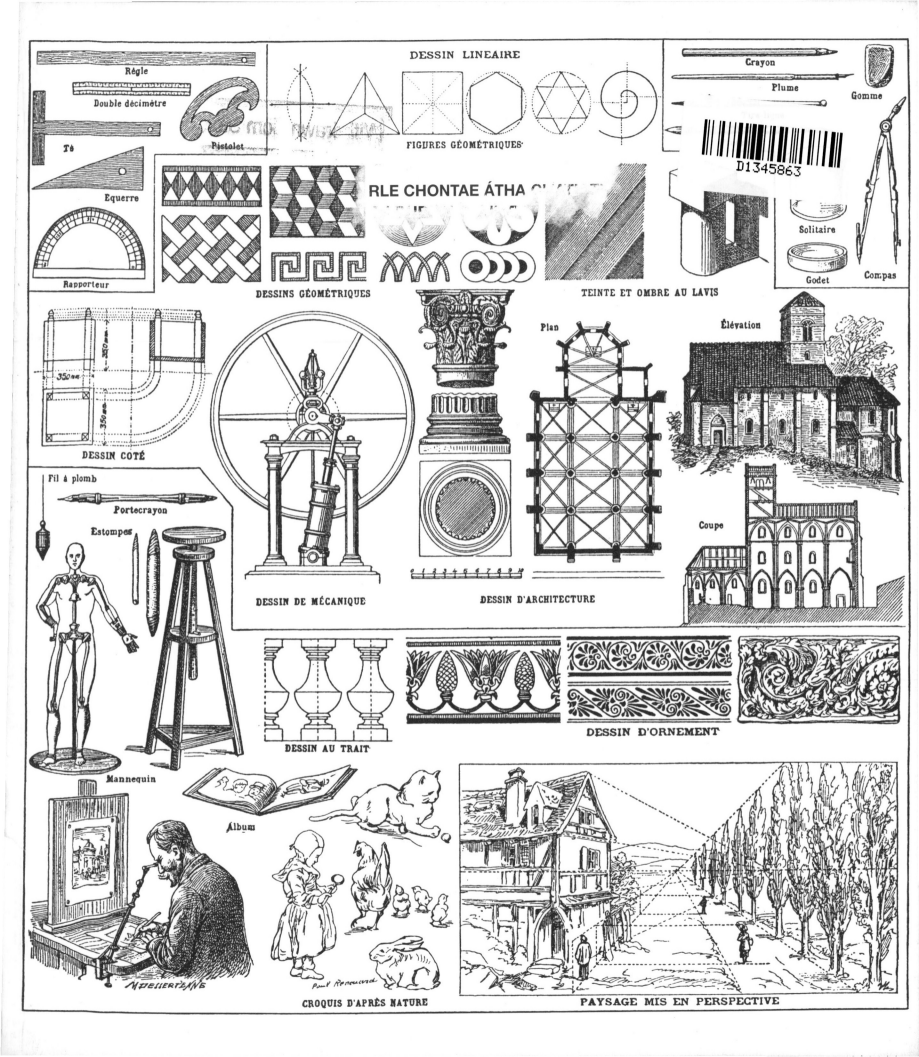

DESSIN LINEAIRE

Régle

Double décimètre

Té

Pistolet

Equerre

FIGURES GÉOMÉTRIQUES

Rapporteur

DESSINS GÉOMÉTRIQUES

TEINTE ET OMBRE AU LAVIS

Crayon

Plume

Gomme

Solitaire

Godet

Compas

DESSIN COTÉ

Fil à plomb

Portecrayon

Estompes

Mannequin

Album

Plan

Élévation

Coupe

DESSIN DE MÉCANIQUE

DESSIN D'ARCHITECTURE

DESSIN AU TRAIT

DESSIN D'ORNEMENT

CROQUIS D'APRÈS NATURE

PAYSAGE MIS EN PERSPECTIVE

TERENCE CONRAN'S
INSPIRATION

Stafford Cliff

INSPIRATION is Terence Conran's most personal book to date. Part visual biography, part guided tour, it lets us look through the keyhole into his home and his work to gain a fascinating insight into the things that motivate and inspire him.

In 1971, when Terence found his 32-room house in Berkshire, it was an almost derelict one-time school. He quickly set about restoring and transforming it into an elegant and spacious family home, and Barton Court has been photographed many times since then, sometimes as a background to furniture catalogues, cookery books and fashion shoots; sometimes for magazine features, TV programmes and interior design books. Recently, Terence has revisited his interior schemes, updating some of his ideas either by changing layouts and replacing fittings or by rethinking furniture and finishes. At the same time, some of the rooms have remained virtually the same for three decades, a testament to the enduring unity of Terence's design philosophy.

Unlike many designers, Terence's style has never been completely modern nor completely traditional, but a unique combination of the two. This has always been his hallmark, an inspired juxtaposition of old and new, stylish and quirky, serious and humorous, functional and decorative; a style that was evident even in the first Habitat shop when it opened in 1964. Nowhere is this clearer than in Terence's own home.

Exploring Barton Court now, as this book does, its rooms can be seen as the repository of a lifetime of ideas and experiences. Like the scrapbooks Terence keeps, the objects, furniture and paintings they contain help to build a picture of his distinctive approach to design. All his things have a history, many are beautiful, some are surprising. His collections have provided – and continue to provide – the inspiration for much of his work and as such can be seen as the source of his creativity. But what is creativity? Perhaps one of its most important elements is keeping our eyes open and learning how to look. Terence's talent is to see the beauty in simple things and the simplicity of some of the most beautiful, whether it be a piece of laboratory glass or a Dutch still-life. He finds inspiration just as often in utilitarian industrial objects as in the forms and colours of nature and, as you leaf through these pages, you will begin to see the world with new eyes.

Whatever you take from this book, you will discover why Terence Conran's life and work have been such a singular and consistent example to our age, and why his belief in intelligent design and the way it can improve the quality of our everyday lives is still an inspiration to millions.

the house

There are many rather sentimental descriptions of home: 'Home sweet home',
'Home is where the heart is'. All are true in my case.

My home is fundamentally important to me, mainly because it is where my family live and gather together, and also because it is the place in which I feel most relaxed and content. Here I have the time and space to think, and I am surrounded by the things that inspire me.

Perhaps I had better describe it for you. Barton Court is a large redbrick house, built in 1772 and once lived in by Charles Dundas, 1st Baron Amesbury, a liberal politician and Chairman of the Kennet and Avon Canal Company. The canal is fed by the River Kennet, which flows just in front of the house, and is still well used, these days for pleasure rather than industry. The first time I saw Barton Court, I liked it primarily because it was Georgian and I love the symmetry and restraint of this style; and secondly, because of the water meadows and the proximity to the river. When I bought it, the house was in a totally derelict state. I had to organize a major rebuilding programme as the roof had fallen in and the whole place was seething with that horrible disease called dry rot, which attacks wood, brick and plaster. This was good in one way, as it meant that most of the period features had been destroyed and I was not bothered by conservation officers wanting me to restore the house to its eighteenth-century splendour. I could make it simple and modern. The proportions of the rooms and the space made a perfect twentieth-century home.

The most ambitious thing I did was to create an 80-foot living room along the front of the house by taking out two walls. The builders told me that it was going to cost a fortune, and I didn't have much money at the time, but there was no question of not doing it. I was right to push ahead because it is now a spectacular space. The only other major structural change I made was to remove the servants' staircase so that I could put in four bathrooms on the upper floors. As in all Georgian houses, though, the elegant simplicity of the layout meant that few alterations were needed and most rooms just required a coat of white paint. There were some places where the ceiling mouldings or fireplaces were still good, so I repaired and retained these, as I have always thought that a mixture of old and new works well, if it is well balanced and carefully done. The whole renovation process was a great learning experience. I discovered a lot about heating, plumbing, woodworking and electrical installation, and also the cost and complexity of doing such an enormous job, all of which has stood me in good stead.

Outside, I moved the main entrance from the front of the house to the rear because I thought it was a shame that the south-facing aspect was taken up with cars sitting in the drive. I made a raised garden here, which gave the house some privacy and helped to ground it in the landscape – when I first saw Barton Court, it looked a bit like a large dolls' house that had been dropped down in a field.

One of the greatest pleasures that came with the house was an enormous walled garden and orchard. Both were filled with Christmas trees and six-foot-high thistles, and one of my first tasks was to root them out and create a very large kitchen garden, with soft fruit and an abundant variety of vegetables. I also restored the various greenhouses and the conservatory, which were as derelict as the house. The vegetable garden is now immensely productive thanks to the energy and skill of Jonathan Chidsey, our gardener.

Another considerable advantage of the property was a series of derelict farm buildings that had held the animals from a prosperous but failing dairy farm. When I was running Habitat, I decided that the stable building would make an ideal design studio and workshop in which to build prototypes of the products we designed, because it was near the Habitat head office and warehouse. This worked extremely well for about eight years until the team moved back to join the rest of the Conran designers in the Heal's building in London. However, these old buildings remain a place of creative enterprise.

I personally feel very at home in this area of west Berkshire as my paternal family lived just the other side of Kintbury, our nearest village, on a huge estate called West Woodhay. They were called Sloper and were the Newbury members of parliament; I still have their family portraits, which I rather treasure. My grandmother and my father lived in the house in West Woodhay in the 1920s, but it was sold when the stockmarkets crashed. I am told that they once owned the land on which my house is built, but that may be a sentimental myth.

21

M.VW

Bonneval,

1953

Conran
a
Bonneval

living

I have always maintained that how and where we live has a profound effect on our wellbeing and creativity.

As you will see, my home life has a sort of synergy that I guess is fairly unusual. I have never been happy with the idea of dividing one's time into work and pleasure; this seems intrinsically impractical and somewhat stressful. For me, a well-ordered, comfortable home is the answer, somewhere I can relax and be productive at the same time.

I love being able to work when I want to and have the tools of my trade to hand. My house is a calm place that allows me the psychological freedom to think, design and write. It is filled with all the books I need for reference and the models of my designs, plus my own private museum of objects and artworks that I have collected over the years. Most of these are simple things that have no value except to me, but I find them a constant source of inspiration. I also keep huge scrapbooks of photographs I have taken or things I have seen in various magazines. They act as *aide-mémoires* for meetings on future directions with the shop buyers and designers. If I get stuck on a project, I will go through my scrapbooks and look at and read books from my library, or maybe just flick through the latest batch of magazines that have arrived in profusion on my work table. A walk in the garden often helps, too, and a bench seat by the river looking at the water can set the thought process flowing again – especially with a glass of wine and a cigar.

My current office at Barton Court is a large space above the kitchen where there is room for my PA and design assistant. When I am working on a new design, I first sketch out ideas on an A4 layout pad and then explain these to my design assistant, who puts them on to computer. I will then probably correct some proportion or discuss the method of construction before he finishes the CAD drawing. Only when we have made a tenth-scale model of the product will I know if we have reached a viable solution. If it is a goer, my assistant will then build a fairly crude full-size prototype and at this stage I will be able to make final corrections to the proportions. If it still looks good, we will discuss materials and manufacturing methods and then go to a full-size working prototype. The final test is simply what it feels like. Ergonomics is almost everything. With an interior design, I like to make a white-card scale model of the space and look at it from different angles, gradually deciding on finishes and colours, furniture and lighting, always considering how well the space will work in reality.

A great luxury of my home is that I can use it as my laboratory. When I get a prototype of a piece of furniture or, say, a rug, I can put it into the living room or bedroom and see how it looks and performs in real life. I also get the unbiased opinion of the household, which can provide valuable insights – with some encouragements and some disappointments.

My old office in the stable building is now used as a showroom for Benchmark, the woodworking company that Sean Sutcliffe and I founded in 1983. Benchmark has expanded enormously over the past 20 years and now fills all the renovated farm buildings. We design and make furniture for The Conran Shop and interiors for restaurants, hotels and shops around the world. I love the industrious energy that has replaced the old farm. Benchmark is now the largest employer in the Kintbury area and a visit there to see the myriad projects under construction can be very inspiring. I love factories, as I have always been concerned with the practical aspects of design, and manufacturing methods and new materials often serve as useful catalysts for new ideas.

Food – growing, cooking and eating it – is another essential element of this 'home life'. My wife is a knowledgeable and excellent cook and we will often discuss the menu for a new restaurant. She will then prepare a big list of dishes that we believe are suitable for the new place and the chef will come down to stay for a few nights and cook through the prototype menu. We will taste the food and correct recipes, and the chef can discuss produce with the gardener so we can grow anything that is not generally available. We also have a pretty good wine cellar and we will often arrange a wine tasting so we can match wines with the appropriate foods. These are all-important stages in opening a new restaurant or café and all part of the productive style of our home. This integrated approach to home and work life means that one is never stifled by the other, there is always some kind of balance and, for me, that is the key to a happy, easy existence.

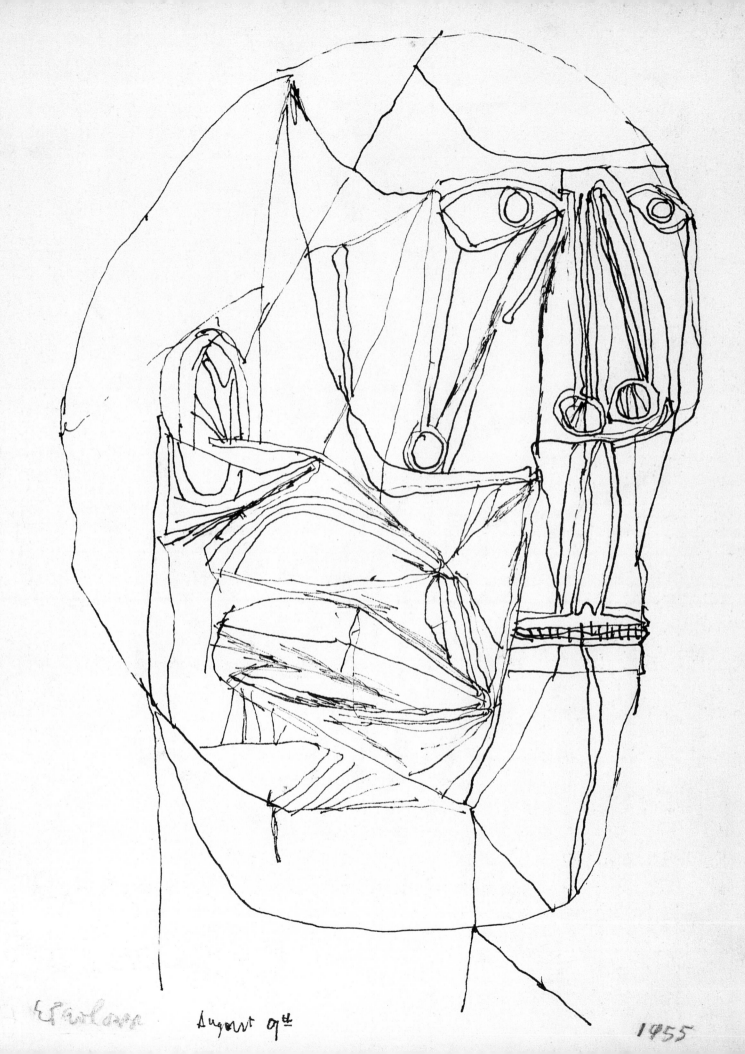

42   Paslarr   August 9th   1955

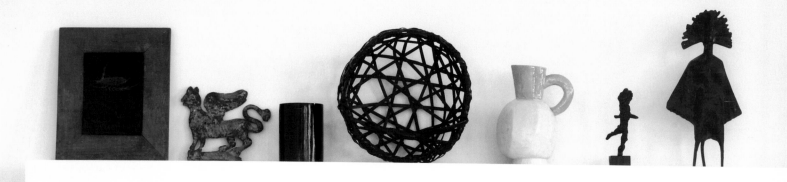

CONRAN FURNITURE

Obtainable at leading stores throughout the British Isles

Shown above, C.7 upholstered Dunlopillo easy chair in various colours, £15. 15. 0d. C.8 cane chair with cushion in bright colours, £9. 0. 0d. P.5 conical plant pot and holder, 14. 0d.

22 PICCADILLY ARCADE, LONDON, W.1
Hyde Park 9210

Wholesale only: FINMAR LIMITED, 12-16 HOLBEIN PLACE, SLOANE SQUARE, LONDON, S.W.1

SWEDISH STAINLESS

700 THEBE

FINMAR

GENSE CUTLERY

KNOWLES

Two's Company . . .

with PLAYER'S Nº 3

PLAYER'S Nº 3
20 Pieces
Extra Quality Cigarettes

The Quality

Cigarette

[3P 121]

This Furniture designed by Terence Conran is strong, well made, surprisingly cheap, and available at most leading stores. Catalogues will be sent upon application.
Sole manufacturers and distributors of conical plant pots and holders.
Approximate retail prices of furniture shown in the above photograph : Conical plant pot and holder (P.3) £1.8.6. Canvas and metal Tripolina chair in red, orange, green, etc., £6.16.0. 5' long coffee table, ash top (T.6) £8.9.6. Stacking table with beech top (T.4) £1.15.0. Dunlopillo upholstered dining chair, various colours (C.4) £6.16.0.

CONRAN FURNITURE
22 Piccadilly Arcade, S.W.1   HYDe Park 9210

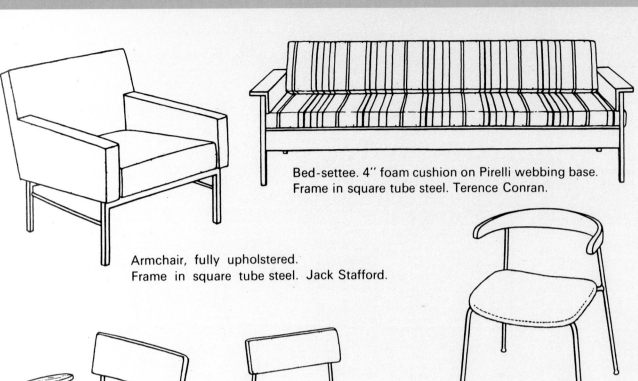

Bed-settee. 4″ foam cushion on Pirelli webbing base. Frame in square tube steel. Terence Conran.

Armchair, fully upholstered. Frame in square tube steel. Jack Stafford.

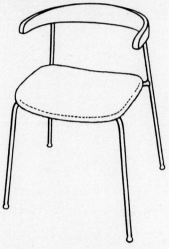

Stacking chair with beech back and upholstered seat. Frame in ¾″ diameter steel tube. Terence Conran.

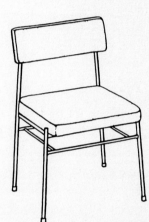

Dining chair with upholstered seat and back. Frame in round tube steel. Jack Stafford.

Dining chair with upholstered seat and back. This chair has solid teak arms and the frame is in round tube steel. Jack Stafford.

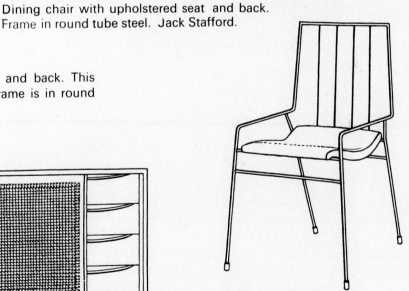

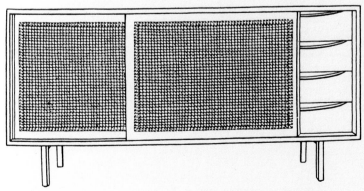

Sideboard in African walnut, sliding door in French cane, legs in 1″ square tube. Terence Conran.

Occasional chair in solid rod with upholstered seat. Designed by Jack Stafford and made by Stafford Furniture Limited.

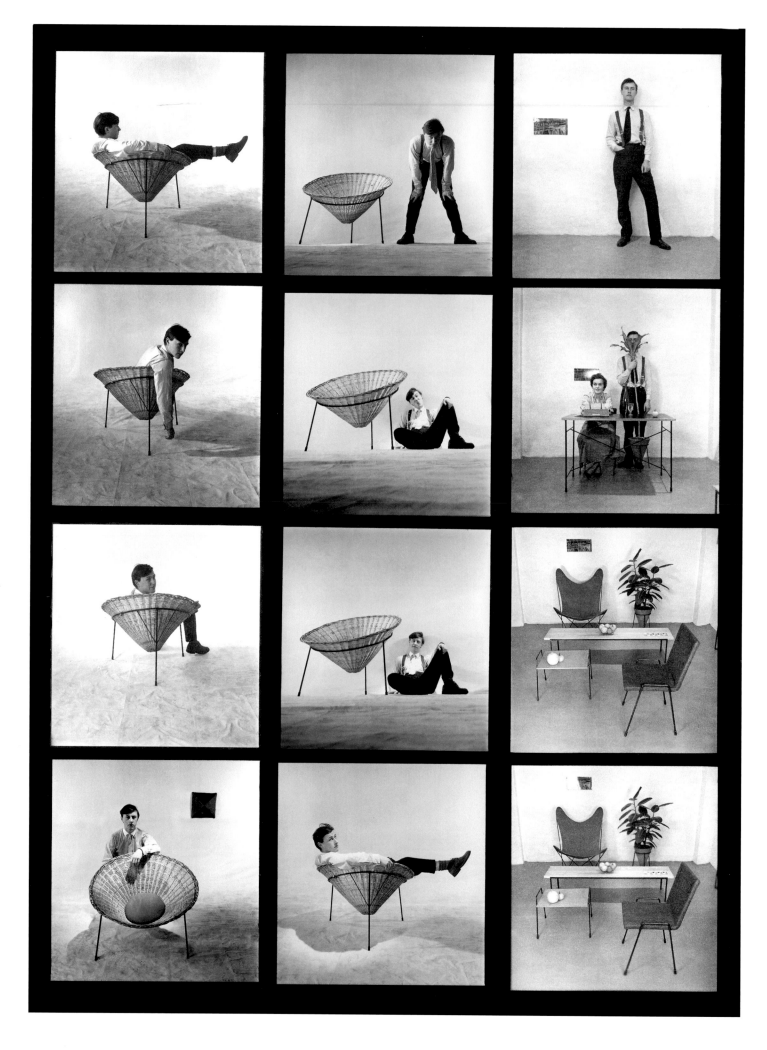

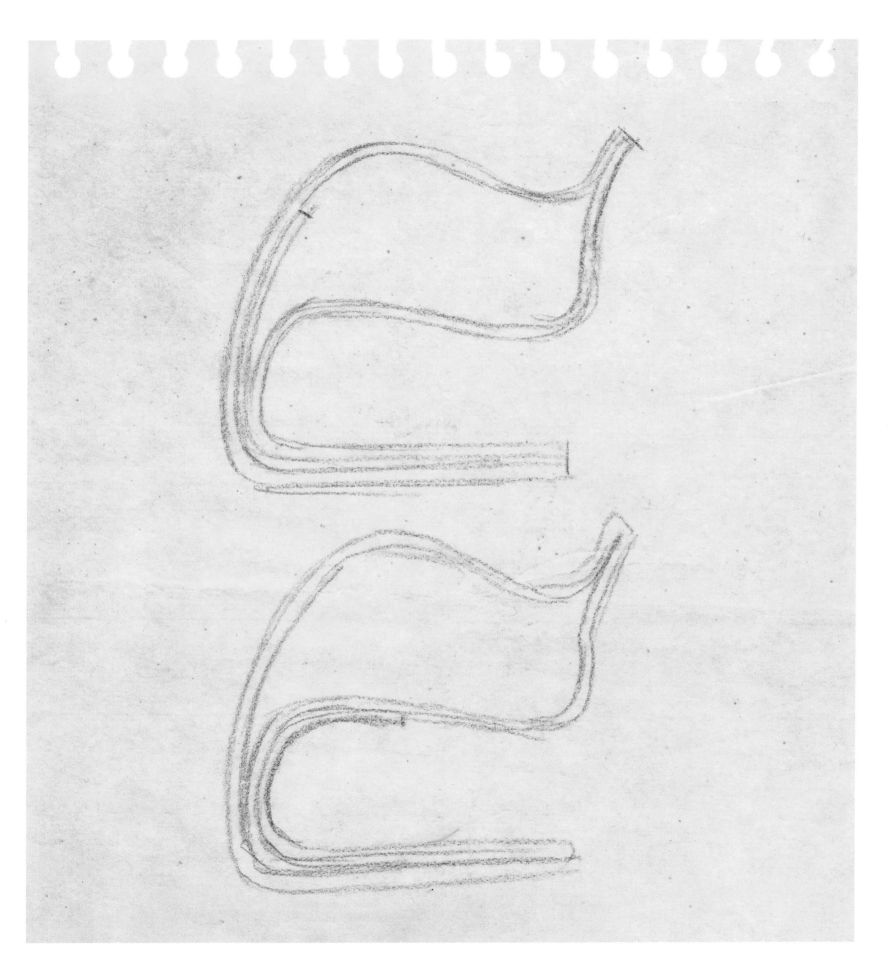

Terence Conran, Habitat and the Design Unit have left Hanway Place and moved to their new home in Covent Garden. Happy New Year.

28 Neal Street London WC2 Telephone 836 2377

cooking

There are certain similarities between design and cooking: both processes involve a creative transformation that produces immensely rewarding results.

Both the pleasure you get from presenting a finished design to your customer or client and the pleasure of putting a good plate of food in front of someone are extremely gratifying, and even better when they really appreciate it. Whether I am designing a new chair or planning a new dish for one of my restaurants, good-quality materials and simple execution are what I believe in. That is not to say that either can be accomplished without expertise and creative thought, but the end result should never feel contrived or tricksy. The most important thing is the natural quality of the raw material, so when it comes to cooking, complex, competing flavours are not for me. As far as I am concerned, fresh ingredients should be allowed to speak for themselves.

I like to cook, but find I rarely have the time. When I do, I make decisions about what to eat based on what the shops, market or garden has to offer, and this can take a whole morning. I get more of an opportunity to cook when we are on holiday and time is not at such a premium. I find French and Italian markets where food shopping is almost as good as eating, particularly seductive – you eat with your eyes and nose. That is why I love markets, though the Grand Epicerie on rue du Bac in Paris is the best food shop I know. In this country it is good to see the growing demand for local produce and the new enthusiasm for farmers' markets. It seems a shame to me that so many people have become disconnected from the food they eat, relying as they do on air-freighted vegetables and shrink-wrapped meat. Rediscovering the texture, taste and smell of ripe seasonal fruit and vegetables would I am sure be a revelation to many. Television programmes are doing a lot to educate people and I think chefs like Jamie Oliver and Hugh Fearnley-Whittingstall are really pushing things in the right direction. I also find their unpretentious approach to cooking very refreshing.

I much prefer simple food that doesn't require lengthy preparation. Cooking from scratch need not be a time-consuming affair and the rewards more than justify the small effort involved. For me, cooking has always been a pleasure, not a chore. I like preparing vegetables and one of my favourite things is a large dish of steamed spring vegetables: peas, broad beans, haricot beans, courgettes, artichokes and asparagus. When served with a large piece of steamed halibut, turbot or cod and a bowl of aïoli, they make a superb summer lunch. I also like to prepare *bagna càuda* with an array of raw vegetables to dip into the delicious hot anchovy sauce. Roast meats are another favourite – a *gigot d'agneau* is one I particularly love, especially if the lamb is very young. In our house in France I had an outdoor grill and, like many men, I really like to cook over a wood fire. Grilled, marinated rabbit is my speciality but, in my opinion, any meat benefits from being cooked in this way.

Restaurant cooking is very different from domestic cooking: the pace is faster, the heat much more intense and the atmosphere frequently frenetic. You need a large dose of adrenalin to work in a busy professional kitchen. One thing it does teach you is to plan ahead and clear up as you go along– plus, above all, the vital importance of timing, which is something every domestic cook should learn. I have always thought that if I had not been a designer, I could well have chosen to be a chef. There is something about the combination of instinct and manual dexterity required to produce the perfect dish that I find very appealing, and the long hours would never have put me off.

One of the things I really like about cooking is the equipment that goes with it: sturdy pots, pans and casseroles, wooden spoons, ceramic bowls and platters, and cast-iron Aga ovens and steel hobs. Everything has to be practical, useful and tough, which means that it has to be intelligently designed. I find a set of good sharp knives much more useful than any complicated gadgets. Basic kitchen equipment is all most of us really need and, of course, it is the simple tasks of chopping vegetables, beating eggs, sifting flour, that make cooking so enjoyable and rewarding in the first place.

At home I like to bring the cooking pot I have used to the table, as it keeps the food hot much longer and is more relaxed than formal tableware. I think there should be an easy connection between cooking and eating, which is why I prefer the kitchen to be open to the dining area. With only a slight rethink, cooking can become part of the satisfying rhythm of daily life and the kitchen less of a place of toil, and more like the heart of the home.

459. Hal. $\frac{1}{2}$.

452. Sk. $\frac{1}{2}$.

454. Boh. $\frac{1}{1}$.

453 a—c. Ö. G. $\frac{2}{3}$.

455 a—c. Sk. $\frac{1}{2}$.

456 a, b. Sk. $\frac{1}{1}$.

460. Sk. $\frac{1}{2}$.

457 a, b. Ö. G. $\frac{1}{2}$.

444. Sk. $\frac{1}{1}$.

458 a, b. Bl. $\frac{1}{1}$.

450. Sk. $\frac{1}{1}$.

445. Sk. $\frac{1}{1}$.

446. Boh. $\frac{1}{1}$.

447. V. G. $\frac{1}{1}$.

461. Sk. $\frac{1}{2}$.

462. Sk. $\frac{1}{2}$.

463. Sm. $\frac{2}{3}$.

448. Dal. $\frac{1}{1}$.

449. Boh. $\frac{1}{1}$.

451. V.G. $\frac{1}{2}$.

464 a, b. Vbtn. $\frac{1}{1}$.

465. Upl. $\frac{1}{2}$.

466. Sk. $\frac{1}{2}$.

467. Sk. $\frac{1}{2}$.

468. Sk. $\frac{1}{2}$.

469. Sk. $\frac{1}{2}$.

470. Sk. $\frac{1}{2}$.

3 Rue St Martial Angoulême

MATÈRIEL DE CUISINE

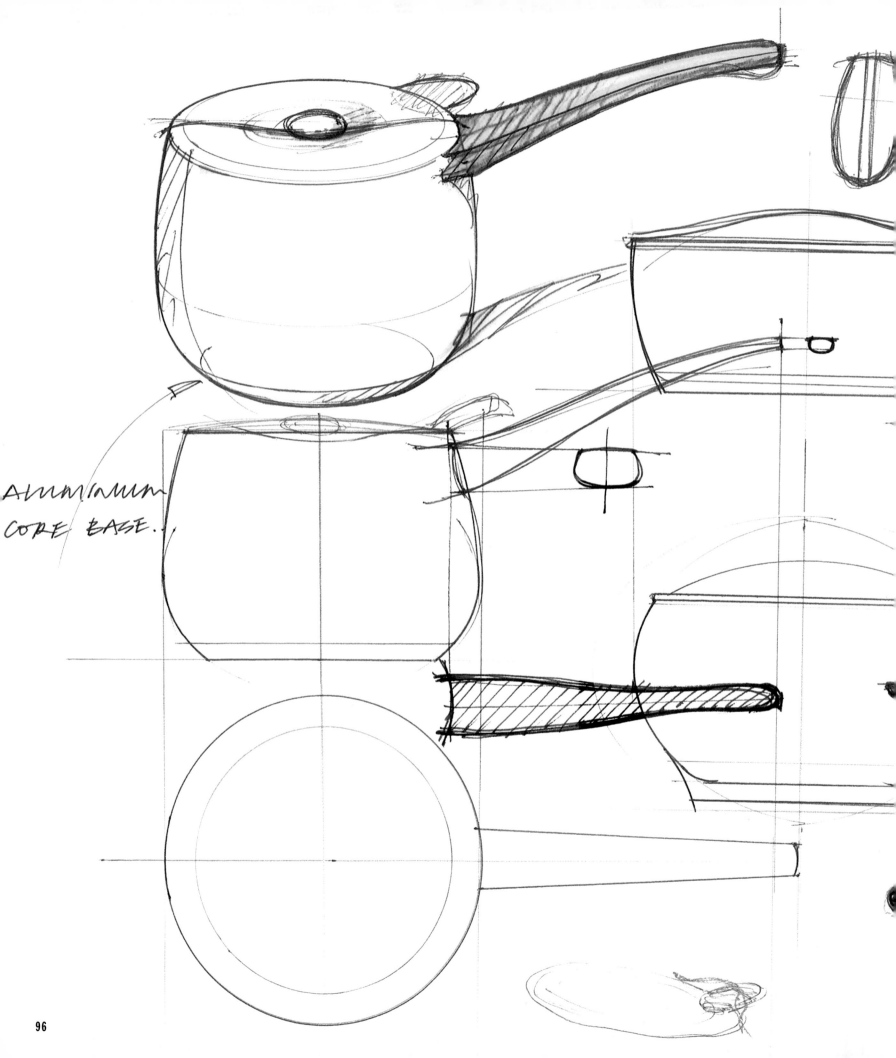

ALUMINIUM
CORE BASE.

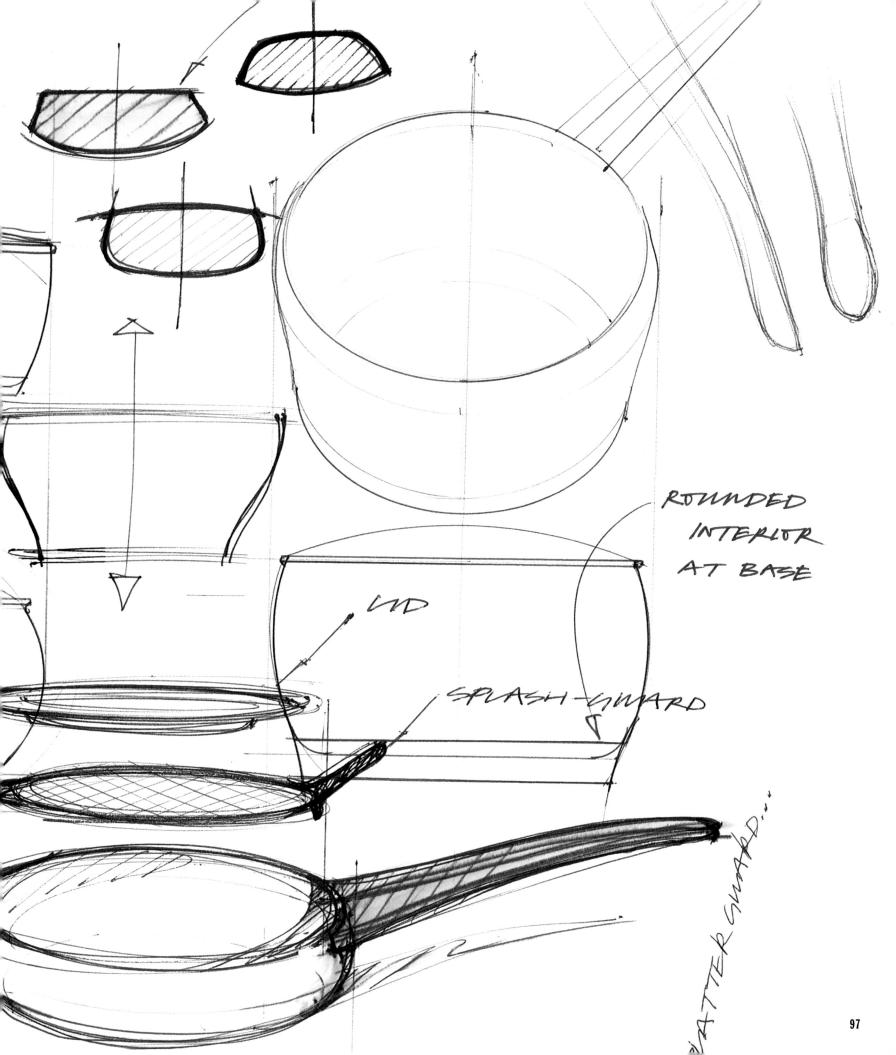

ROUNDED
INTERIOR
AT BASE

LID

SPLASH-GUARD

SPATTER GUARD...

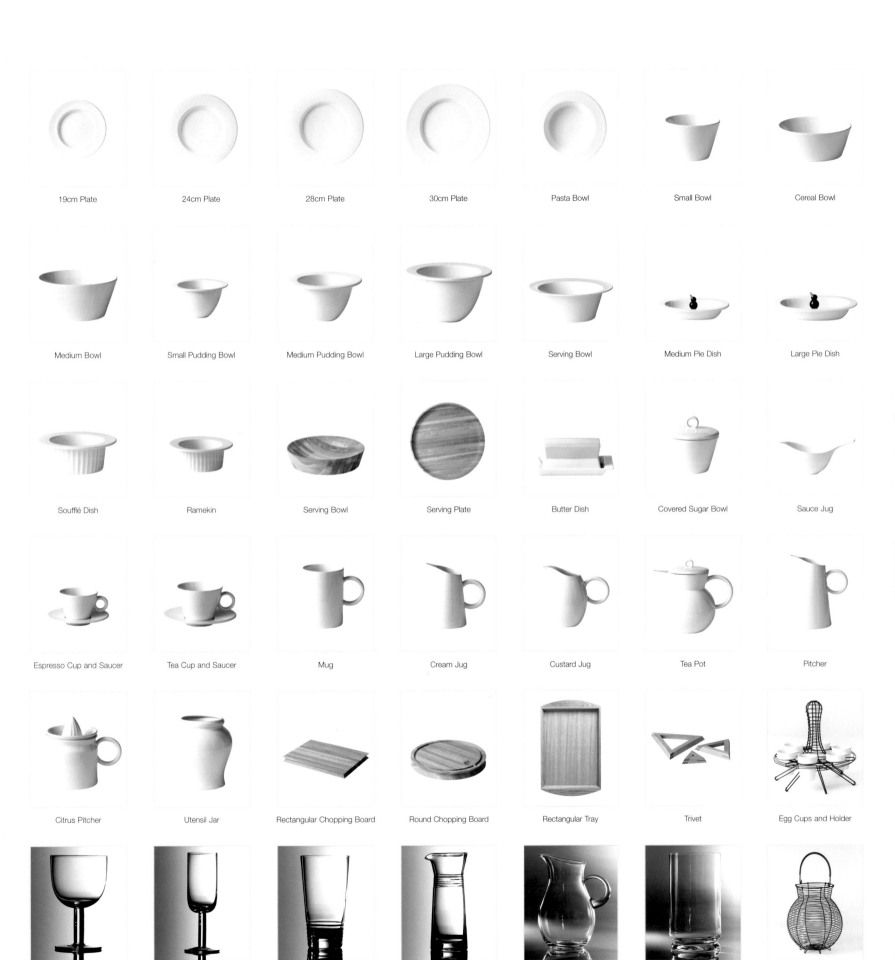

19cm Plate	24cm Plate	28cm Plate	30cm Plate	Pasta Bowl	Small Bowl	Cereal Bowl
Medium Bowl	Small Pudding Bowl	Medium Pudding Bowl	Large Pudding Bowl	Serving Bowl	Medium Pie Dish	Large Pie Dish
Soufflé Dish	Ramekin	Serving Bowl	Serving Plate	Butter Dish	Covered Sugar Bowl	Sauce Jug
Espresso Cup and Saucer	Tea Cup and Saucer	Mug	Cream Jug	Custard Jug	Tea Pot	Pitcher
Citrus Pitcher	Utensil Jar	Rectangular Chopping Board	Round Chopping Board	Rectangular Tray	Trivet	Egg Cups and Holder
Red Wine Glass	Flute	Hiball	Carafe	Carafe	Hurricane Lamp	Basket

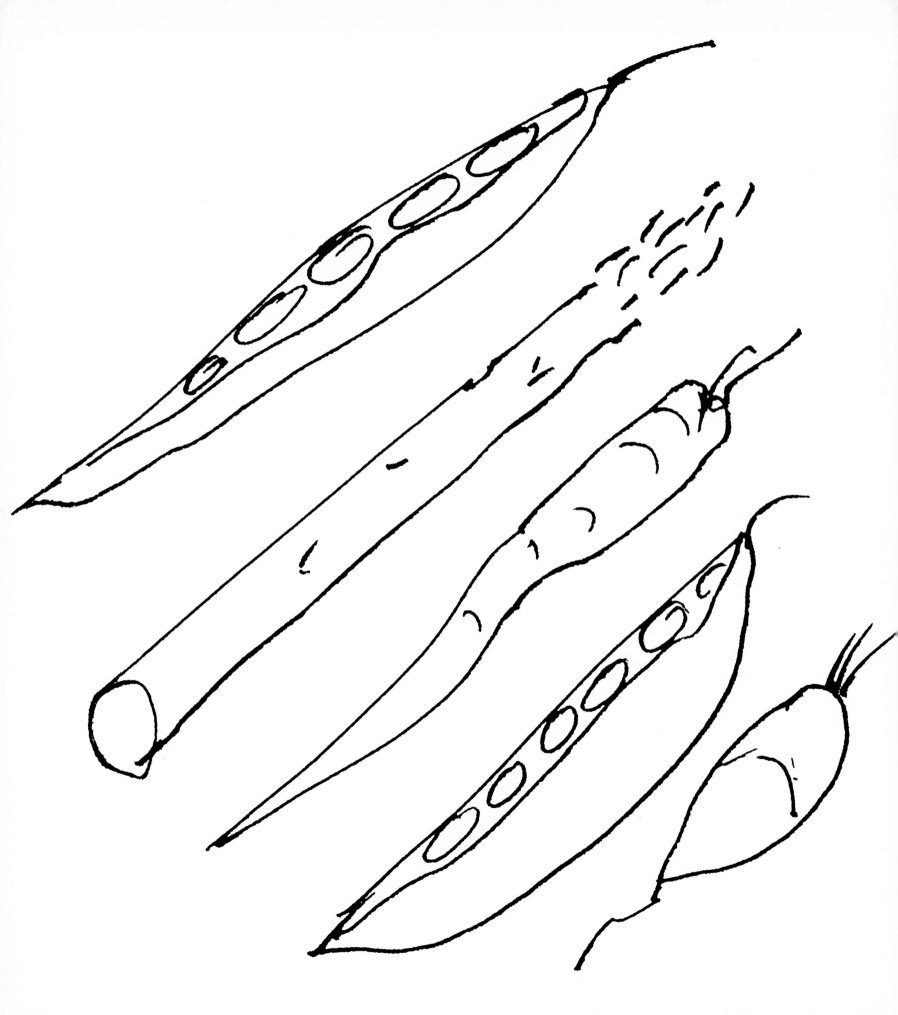

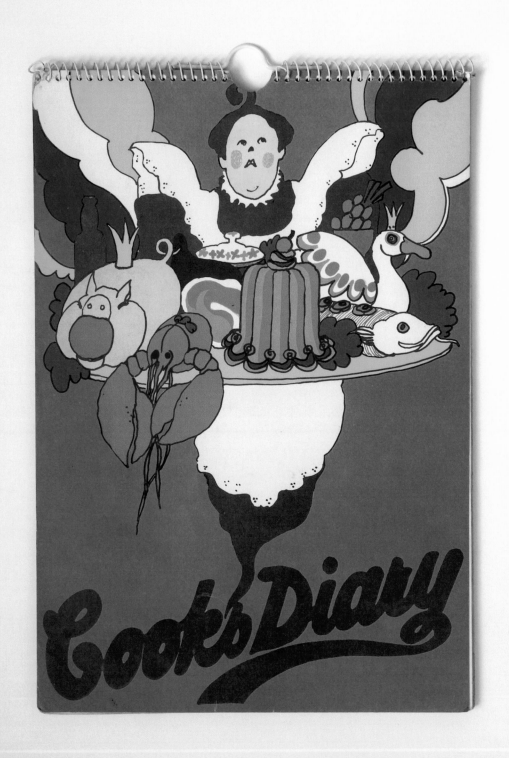

eating

One of my greatest pleasures is a good lunch with convivial company, plenty of wine and no pressing problems to solve in the afternoon.

There should always be time for eating and talking, which is why I love France, where this is taken as a matter of course.

As a restaurateur, I am particularly aware of the importance of setting and the effect it has on our enjoyment of food. On the whole, I prefer unpretentious surroundings for lunch, such as a brasserie or bistro, and grandeur for dinner – Les Ambassadeurs at the Crillon in Paris, perhaps. Lunchtime food should be simple: an endive and walnut salad, a *choucroute garni* and a bottle of Fleurie is perfect. Nowhere does this better than that wonderful Left Bank institution, Brasserie Lipp, where you sit on *banquettes* at small tables with white tablecloths and plain white bowls and plates. There is a certain honesty to this – I abhor frilly tableware with artfully arranged food surrounded by swirls of sauce and foam. There is a place for *haute cuisine*, however, when it is done well. The last time I ate at Les Ambassadeurs, it was quite delicious, though, curiously, the thing I remember most was a little plate of different butters – one was so tasty that I ate the whole pot of it on some simple French bread.

As far as I am concerned, uncomplicated, classic dishes cannot be surpassed. When it comes to meat, I think offal is often underrated. Veal kidneys split in half, grilled over a fierce fire and served with *sauce béarnaise* are particularly good, and liver, sweetbreads, even *tête de veau* and tripe, are all incredibly tasty. I also like terrines, pâtés and charcuterie; a large plate of these makes an excellent lunch with a bottle of red burgundy and a green salad. A *steak au poivre* is a constant pleasure, but birds are my real favourites. I love anything from a proper chicken, roasted à la Simon Hopkinson, to *anjou* pigeons, snipe, woodcock, pheasant and partridge. My all-time favourite, however, has to be young roast grouse. At Christmas roast goose tastes magnificent, and is much better than turkey, which is actually very dull, with little or no flavour.

Shellfish are another passion. A dish of lightly grilled scallops really gets the gastric juices going and the oyster season is always an excitement – a dozen Whitstable or Colchester oysters make a perfect meal, especially with some rye or soda bread. Scottish langoustines served with a dash of mayonnaise are also excellent, as are Scottish or Cornish lobsters and delicious Norfolk crabs. I love well-smoked kippers, especially for Sunday breakfast, and a plate of finely sliced smoked wild salmon is a treat at any time of day. Turbot is lovely, as is a Dover sole *meunière* or halibut with aïoli and young vegetables. Cod is another fine white fish, but sadly in very short supply these days.

And so I come to vegetables, which are probably my favourite food of all. I suppose my enjoyment of vegetables is partially to do with the fact that we grow them ourselves and when they are fresh from the garden they have incredible flavour. My happiest gardening moment is when the first peas and broad beans are ready to pick. They are perfect eaten raw or simply cooked with a smear of butter. I also adore asparagus and globe artichokes and, later in the year, roasted Jerusalem artichokes are something else to look forward to. Then there are herbs, which have a remarkable impact on any dish – I particularly like the first tarragon with a steamed chicken in the spring. Fine french beans are delicious in salads, and so are the first new potatoes and the waxy midsummer varieties. A tomato salad in September, when the fruit have had enough sun, served with salt, a little garlic and lots of olive oil, is hard to beat. Autumn potatoes make wonderful *pommes lyonnais* and *gratin dauphinoise*, which is especially good with a few slivers of black truffle. Other autumn delicacies are fungi: richly flavoured cèpes and chanterelles, and the common or garden field mushroom, which should never be overlooked.

We have lots of soft fruit in our garden at Barton Court: raspberries, loganberries, strawberries and *fraises du bois*, as well as white, red and blackcurrants for jellies and purées. For me, though, the best berries of all are the autumn Scottish raspberries, which are coloured mellow yellow and taste rather mellow as well. I always enjoy the apple season as there are so many wonderful apple dishes: baked apples is one of my favourites and stewed apples with quinces are delicious, as are *tarte fin* and *tarte Tatin*.

I hope you can sense my enthusiasm for food: it inspires the dishes I cook at home and ones I would like to offer in my restaurants. There are few things more agreeable than a good meal with family and friends, and for me it is an essential component of a happy life.

121

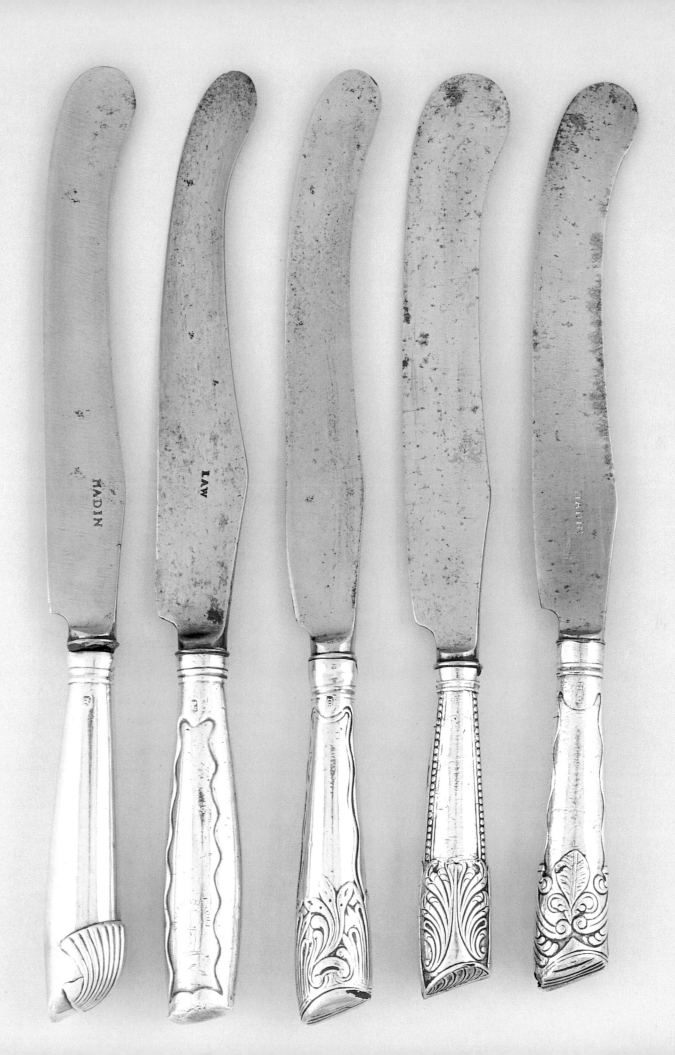

127

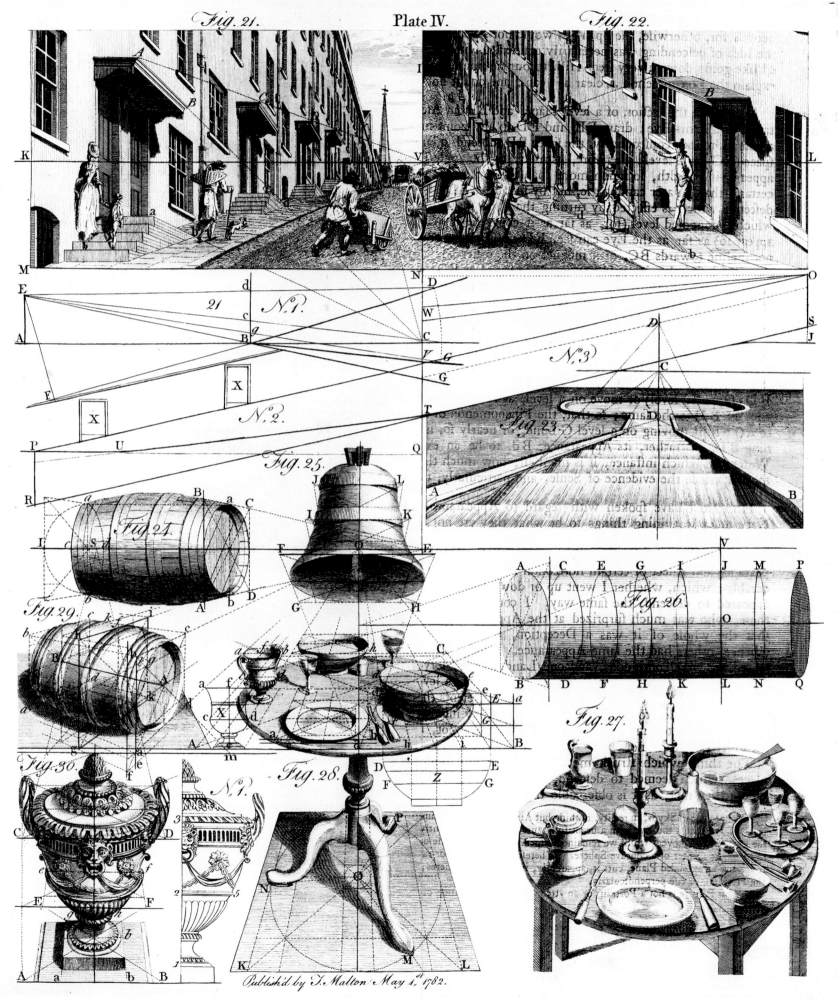

Fig. 21.

Plate IV.

Fig. 22.

Fig. 23.

Fig. 24.

Fig. 25.

Fig. 26.

Fig. 27.

Fig. 28.

Fig. 29.

Fig. 30.

Publish'd by T. Malton May 1.st 1782.

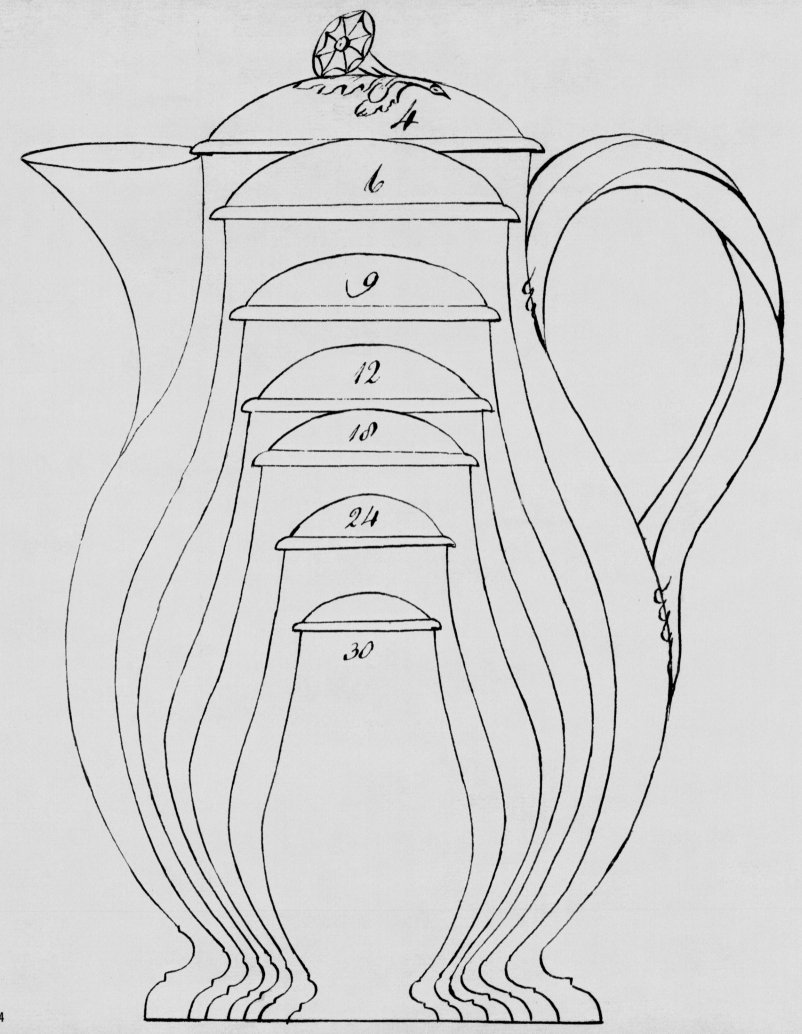

135

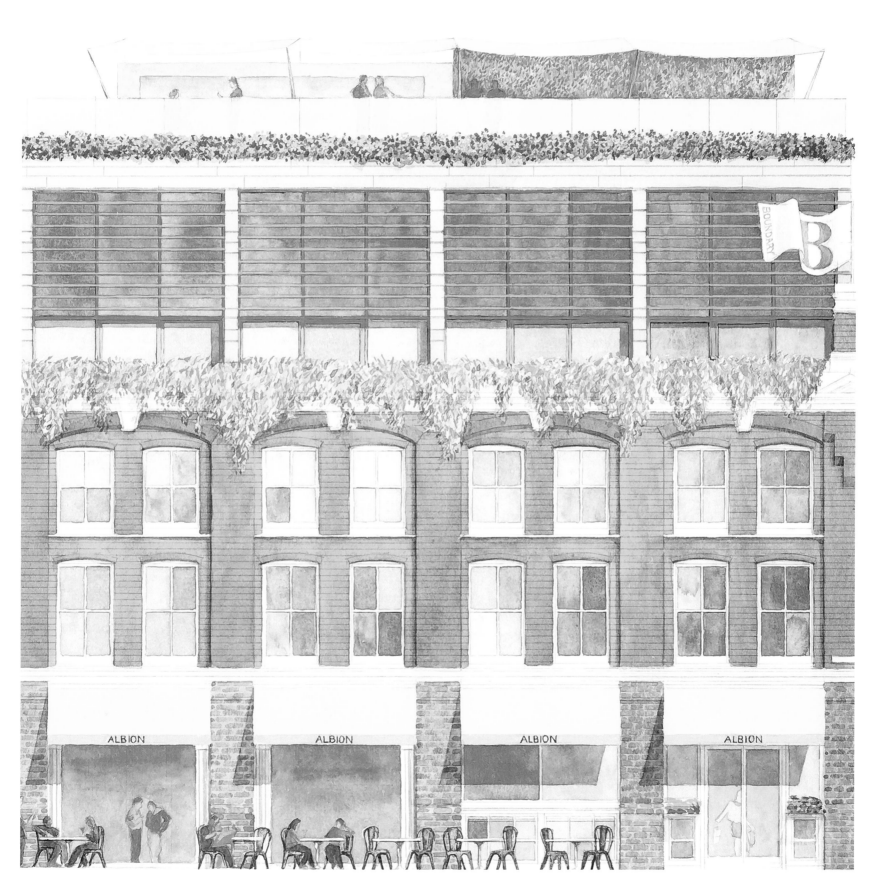

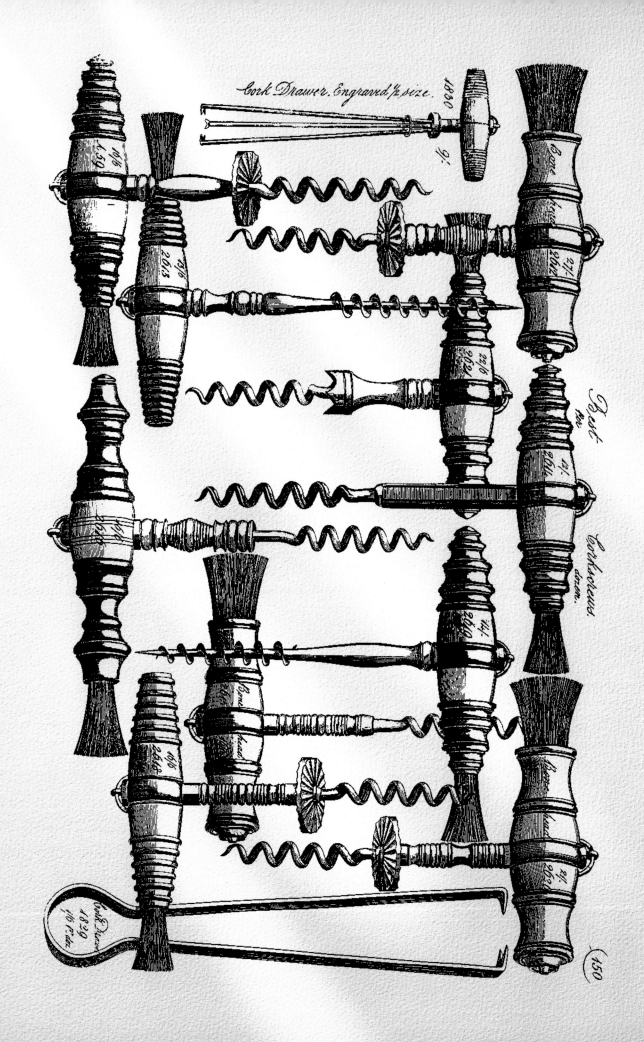

Cork Drawer. Engraved 1/2 size.

150

152

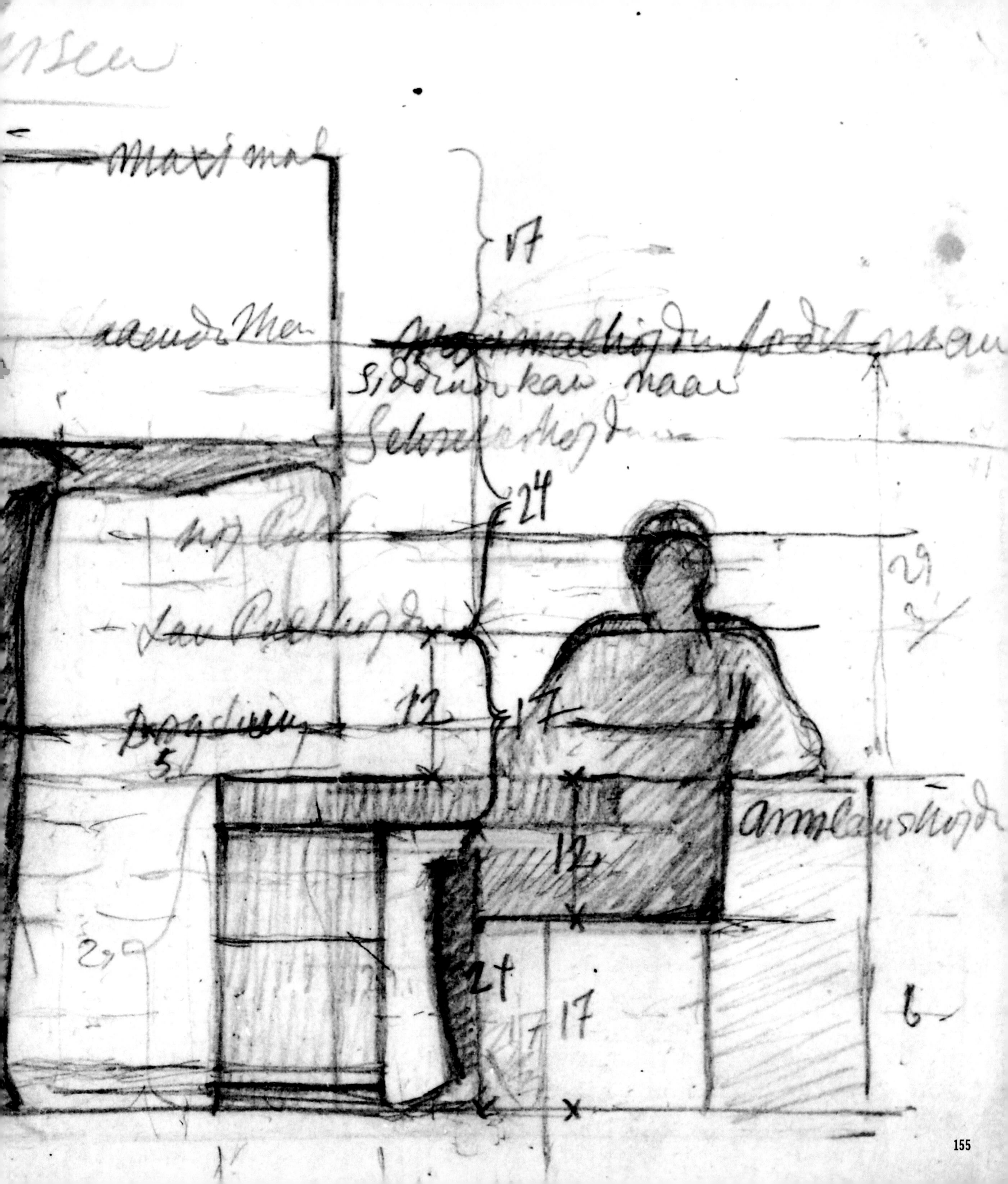
maximal
17
24
12
17
5
29
12
24
17
6

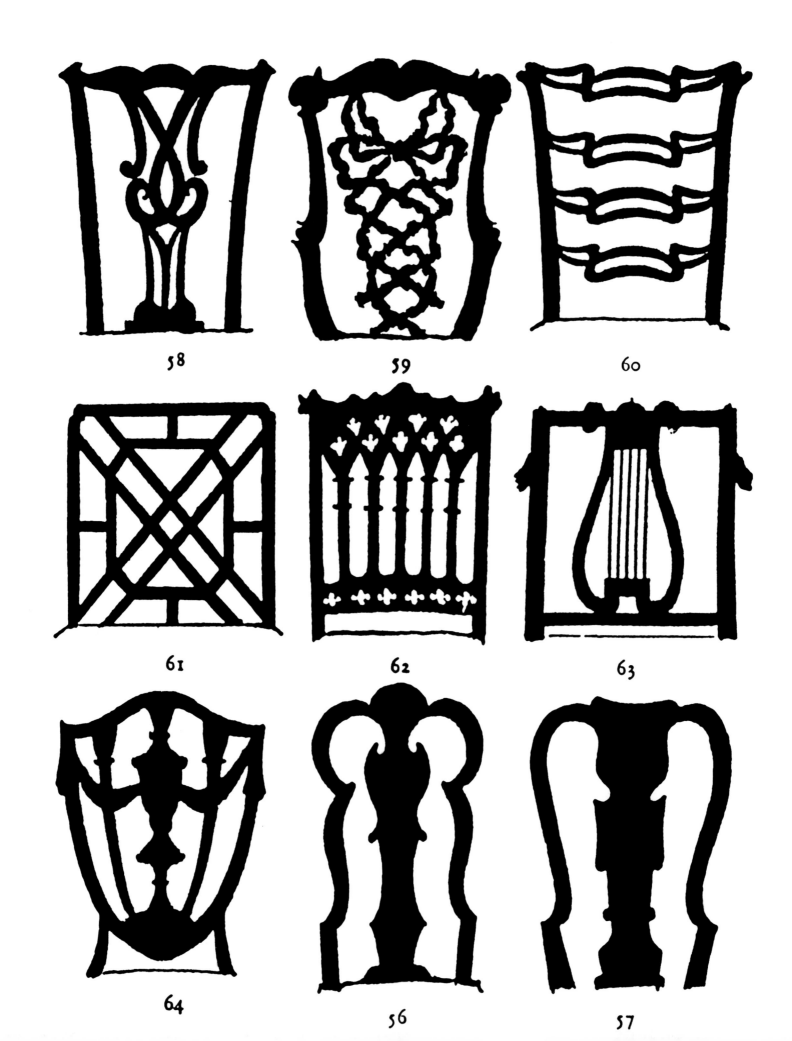

58

59

60

61

62

63

64

56

57

YOUNG & MARTEN, Ltd., Merchants and Manufacturers,

Round Turned Wood Balusters.

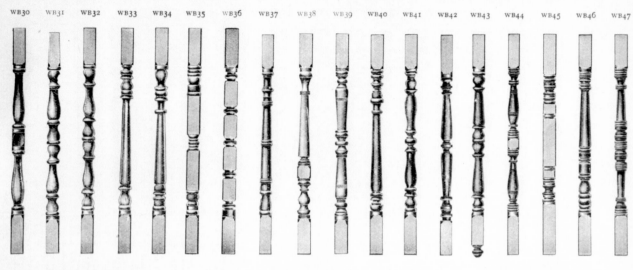

3 ft. long.

Prices, per dozen.

No.	Size.	Deal.	P. Pine.	Mahogany.	Oak.	Walnut.
WB30 to WB34	Ex. 1¼ ins.	1/10½	3/4	6/3	6/3	8/1½
	„ 1½ „	2/3	3/9	7/6	7/6	8/9
	„ 1¾ „	3/1½	5/3	9/6	9/6	12/-
	„ 2 „	3/9	6/3	10/6	10/6	14/6
WB35, WB36, WB37	Ex. 1¼ ins.	2/6	4/-	8/-	8/-	9/6
	„ 1½ „	3/6	5/6	9/9	9/9	12/6
	„ 2 „	4/-	7/-	11/3	11/6	15/-
WB38, WB39	Ex. 1¼ ins.	2/9	4/6	8/-	8/-	9/6
	„ 1½ „	3/9	6/-	9/9	10/-	12/6
	„ 2 „	4/6	7/6	11/3	12/-	15/-
WB40 to WB43	Ex. 1¼ ins.	3/6	5/-	8/-	8/-	9/6
	„ 1½ „	4/6	6/6	10/-	10/6	12/6
	„ 2 „	5/-	8/-	12/6	12/6	14/6
WB44 to WB49	Ex. 1¼ ins.	5/-	7/-	10/-	10/-	11/3
	„ 1½ „	6/3	8/9	12/-	12/6	14/6
	„ 2 „	7/-	10/-	13/9	14/6	17/6
WB50, WB51	Ex. 1¼ ins.	6/3	8/9	11/3	11/3	12/6
	„ 1½ „	7/6	10/-	13/9	14/6	15/6
	„ 2 „	8/-	11/3	15/-	15/6	18/9
	„ 2½ „	9/6	14/-	17/6	18/-	22/-

Prices, per dozen.

No.	Size.	Deal.	P. Pine.	Mahogany.	Oak.	Walnut.
WB53 Spiral Fluted	Ex. 1¼ ins.	3/9	6/3	9/6	10/-	11/3
	„ 1½ „	5/-	8/9	11/3	12/-	13/9
	„ 2 „	6/3	10/-	14/6	15/-	17/6
WB54 Fluted WB55 Octagon	Ex. 1¼ ins.	6/3	8/9	13/-	13/9	15/6
	„ 1½ „	8/-	11/3	15/-	15/6	17/6
	„ 2 „	8/9	12/6	16/3	17/-	20/-
WB56, WB57, WB58 WB59 Octagon	Ex. 1¾ ins.	11/3	13/9	18/9	19/6	20/6
	„ 2 „	12/-	15/-	20/-	20/6	22/6
WB60 to WB64	Ex. 1¾ ins.	13/-	17/6	21/-	22/-	22/6
	„ 2 „	13/9	18/9	22/-	22/6	24/6
	„ 2½ „	17/6	26/3	33/9	35/-	37/6
WB67, WB70	Ex. 2 ins.	15/-	20/-	23/-	24/6	26/3
	„ 2½ „	22/6	26/3	35/-	36/3	40/-
WB73, WB74	Ex. 2 ins.	20/6	26/3	30/-	31/3	33/9
	„ 2½ „	28/9	31/3	40/-	42/6	45/-
	„ 3 „	33/9	40/-	52/6	55/-	57/6
WB75	Ex. 2½ ins.	45/-	50/-	56/3	57/6	60/-
	„ 3 „	47/6	52/6	62/6	65/-	67/6

Where a number of sizes of an individual article are described, the sizes kept in stock are priced in larger letterpress.

sleeping

In the seclusion of the bedroom we can really relax, unwind and be ourselves, and for many of us, our bed is one of our most valued spaces. That is certainly true for me.

I like beds and the intimacy they induce. I like reading and watching television in bed and, in winter, I really enjoy having a log fire in the bedroom. What I love particularly, though, is lying in bed thinking on a sunny Sunday morning – some of my best ideas have been inspired by sunshine and the smell of wisteria on the wall outside. I think it is often the view from the windows and the quality of the light that make a bedroom special. I can remember one particular room I stayed in once in a small hotel on the Italian coast south of Spezia. It had a plain terracotta-tiled floor and a large bed with white cotton sheets. The total simplicity of the room, the smell of the sea, the light in the morning and the noise made by the restaurant below beating chunks of veal into escalopes, made it truly wonderful.

Throughout my life, I have stayed in hundreds of hotel rooms, some better than others. By and large, I tend to prefer traditional old hotels to the modern 'boutique' ones, though I like seeing what people have made of the interiors. Strangely, I don't think I have often slept in a London hotel, though I designed the rooms for the Great Eastern Hotel at Liverpool Street Station when we bought it in 1999. Taking a lead from the businessmen we thought might be staying there, I made them quite tailored, and used pinstriped suiting material on the upholstery. Recently, I have been having a lot of fun designing the bedrooms in the Boundary Road Project. Each one is a homage to a favourite designer of mine: Andrée Putman, Charles Eames, Le Corbusier and Josef Hoffmann; I have even done one in the style of that wonderfully idiosyncratic British illustrator W. Heath Robinson. Vicki has also designed a bedroom and so has my sister Priscilla. The biggest suite has been created by Sir David Tang, in his own style of chinoiserie.

At home practicality and comfort are the most important things to me when it comes to sleeping arrangements. In terms of design, I think it is vital to have proper storage. You cannot create a restful environment if you are surrounded by clutter and a decent-sized wardrobe is vital or, in an ideal world, a dressing room. As for comfort in my opinion, a good-quality mattress is one of the most important purchases you will ever make – if your body is not well supported, you will not get a good night's sleep and even the most elegant bed will have failed in its purpose. Heal's had a long history of manufacturing beds when we took it over in 1983 and I found the construction of mattresses absolutely fascinating. The Heal's ones were made with spun horsehair, a now somewhat old-fashioned material, that nevertheless performs very well. I recently went into a shop in SoHo in New York and was amazed to find that they were selling beds for $20,000. When I thought about it, however, I decided that it was not such a ridiculous idea, providing you have a large budget. After all, you spend roughly a third of your life in bed, so to be perfectly comfortable may be well worth the investment.

For bedlinen, I like very fine white percale cotton or linen sheets that have been dried in the sun. A few years ago, I created 'Bed by Conran', a range of contemporary bedlinen for Dorma. I thoroughly enjoyed working on the project because it took me back to textile design, which is where I began in the 1950s. A large bed is a useful surface for introducing colour and pattern into an interior, whether you choose the subtle shades of a woven bedspread from India or a bright silk throw. Needless to say, I have never been one for those layers of floral display cushions that seem to be popular in house makeover programmes at the moment – it all seems much too fussy.

I am still a big fan of duvets, or 'continental quilts' as they used to be called. We first started selling them in Habitat in 1964 and they were seen as part of the 1960s Free Love revolution. They introduced a more casual feel to the bedroom, formerly the domain of heavy, well-tucked-in blankets, eiderdowns and candlewick bedspreads. Duvets came from Sweden, which at that time had a great reputation for sexual freedom, so they were considered somewhat risqué. In the Habitat catalogue we called the duvet the 'ten-second bed', and photographed a husband making the bed in the morning, while his wife put on her make-up – this caused quite a flurry of comment in the press. But duvets now are probably much more common than sheets and blankets as they make bed-making so much quicker and easier. They are simple and useful, an excellent example of a design innovation that makes a small, positive difference to everyone's lifestyle.

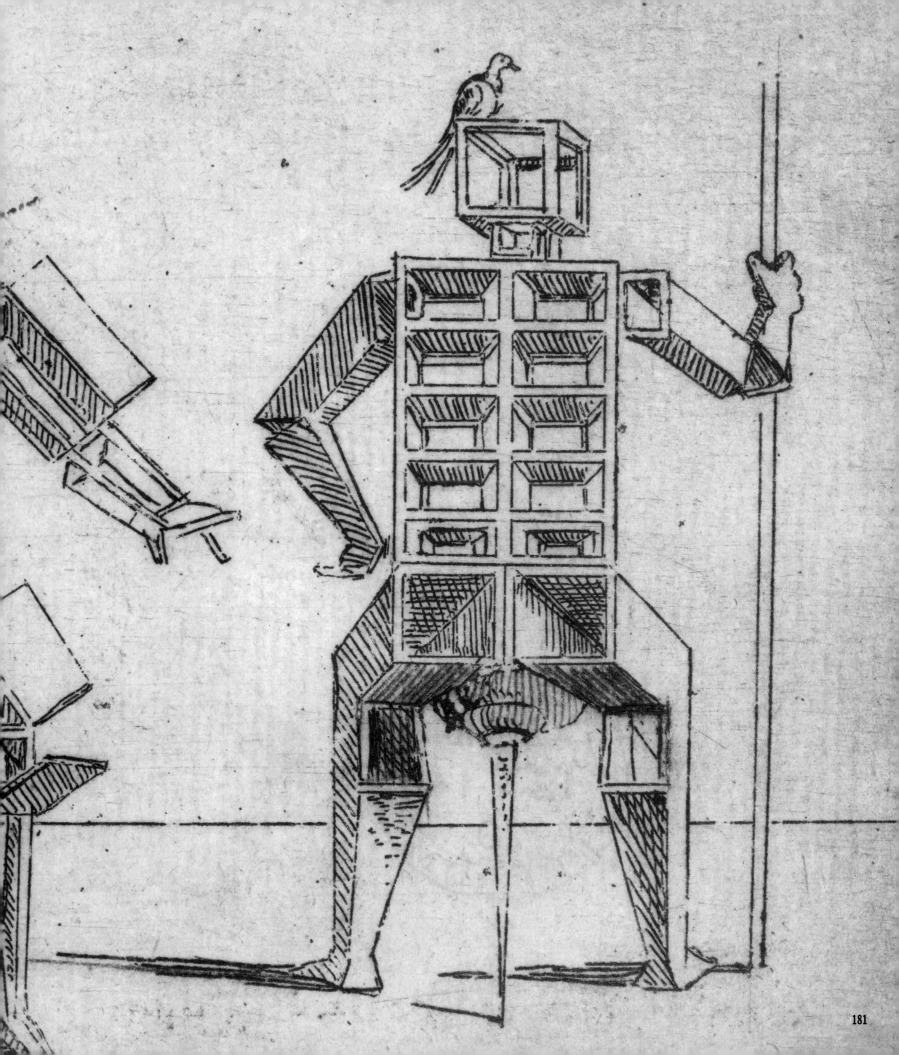

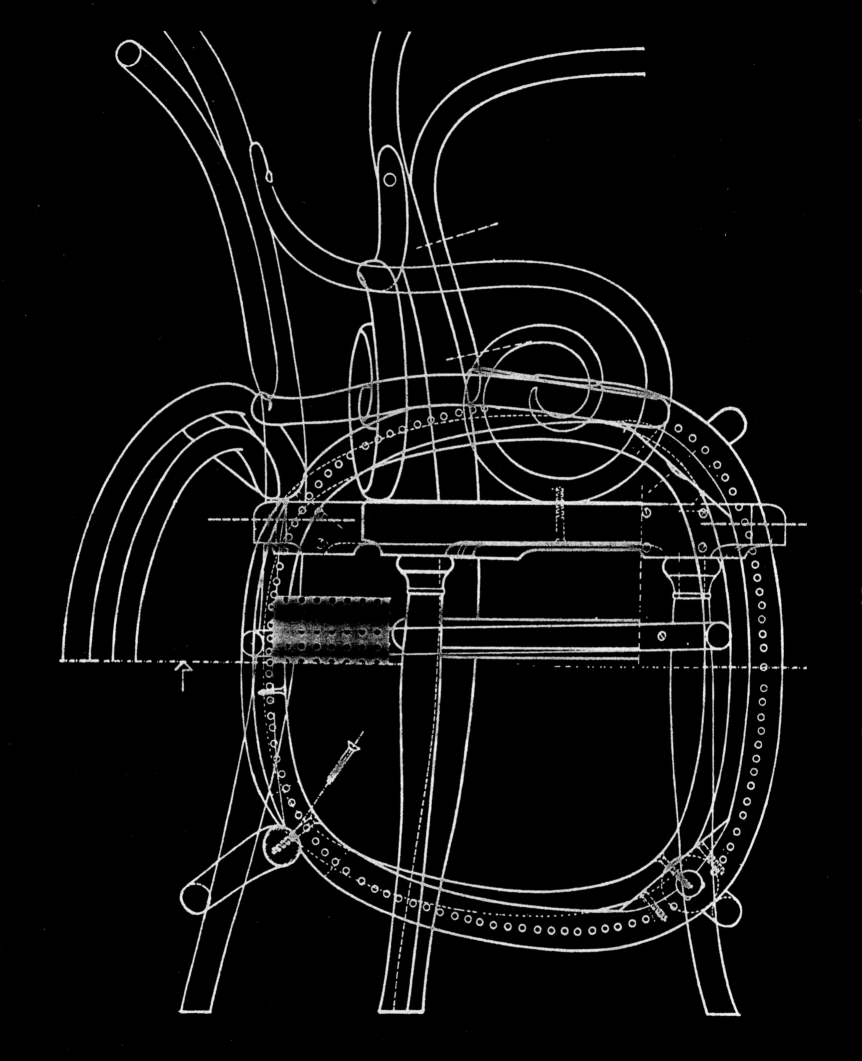

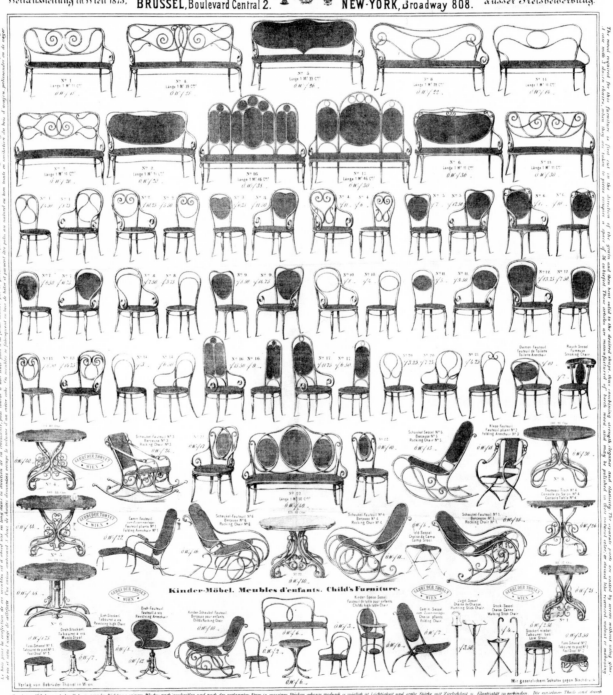

bathing

There is something wonderfully therapeutic and uplifting about being in water, whether you are swimming in the sea or bathing at home.

I love water and find it both relaxing and liberating. Taking a bath is one of my favourite things in life – I have constructive, inspirational thoughts in the bath. It is a place in which I can solve problems and the perfect time to practise a speech or lecture I may have to give later in the day.

A lot of attention is now focused on bathroom design, and over the past ten years or so, good-quality contemporary fittings have become widely available – all in marked contrast to the somewhat perfunctory treatment the bathroom has received in the past. I think this is rather nice, as the bathroom can be a place of sanctuary and relaxation instead of just somewhere to clean your teeth and have a quick scrub down. For designers, bathroom fittings provide a unique opportunity to explore different forms and materials. These days you can choose from sculptural egg-shaped bathtubs and curvaceous loos or barely-there showerheads and minimalist marble basins – I have seen some freestanding basins that look more like artworks than bathroom fittings and would not be out of place in a gallery.

The baths I prefer are reenamelled, cast-iron Victorian monsters with generous taps and hand-held showers. On the whole, I prefer comfort and simplicity. My own shower area at Barton Court is inspired by the concept of the wetroom, where the whole floor area is drained, and water is free to splash about wherever it wants. Natural materials and textures always work well in a bathroom – one of the greatest pleasures we have in our new mews house in London is a heated stone floor, which is delightfully tactile underfoot. Apart from warmth, for me, large, luxurious bath towels are also very important. Above all, I think a bathroom must be somewhere it is a pleasure to spend time.

Trendy new bathrooms photograph extremely well, and property developers and estate agents have fixed on them as an image of sophisticated living and added value. In the same way, the bathroom has become one of the status symbols of some upmarket hotels, with twin basins and even twin tubs becoming ever more common. This probably has less to do with consumer demand and more to do with the aspirations of some hotel designers. I particularly like The Lancaster Hotel in Paris because it has generous baths and simple, spacious marble bathrooms that are not overdressed. Some luxury hotels, however, now offer rather romantic alfresco bathing experiences: in a courtyard open to the jungle; on a platform above the ocean; or on a deck that surveys the African veldt. Although I have never done it, I love the notion of soaking in the tub while elephants amble past or zebras come to drink at a nearby waterhole.

Spas of all kinds are very popular nowadays as well, and you can indulge in almost every kind of water therapy. Japanese wooden baths are wonderful and induce a serene state of mind and smell nice too, but they are not for washing – tradition dictates that you shower before you get into them – they are just for peaceful contemplation. The Jacuzzi, on the other hand, offers a completely different experience, but the results are equally rejuvenating. Scandinavian saunas and Turkish baths are lovely, bringing together as they do the relaxing elements of heat and steam and the invigorating power of cold water. I remember a sauna I had in Finland at a party arranged by Arni Ratia of the textile designers Marimekko many years ago: we all had plenty of Aquavit to drink, got very hot and rushed out and dived into a snow-covered lake. It made me feel marvellous and quite sober!

I very much enjoy swimming pools, especially when they are outside in a warm climate. I like seeing people swimming, swimming myself and watching children really having fun, splashing around with blow-up boats and lilos. I think those infinity pools where the water flows over the edge, making the water level parallel with the ground, are very clever. I once bathed in a pool like this on the side of a hill overlooking the Mediterranean Sea. As you swam along, you experienced the beguiling illusion that the pool and the sea were seamlessly connected. The seaside has long been an inspiration. Fine, sandy beaches, the smell of the sea, the colours of bathing huts and deckchairs, and the shapes of shells, driftwood, yachts, fishing craft and sailboats are all enduring influences. The seaside towns I like best are the ones that have not been messed around with, so still have their original architecture, small cafés and traditional fishing communities. It is very easy to while away days by the sea – what greater happiness is there as a child than pottering about in rock pools, netting shrimps, and collecting shells, fossils and flotsam and jetsam? It is a voyage of discovery.

BROSSES de Charleville, 1re qualité, soie grise et blanche, pour la peinture en bâtiment.
Du N°. 10 compris, ces Brosses se font en soie blanche, ou mêlée de gris et de blanc.

PI. 51.

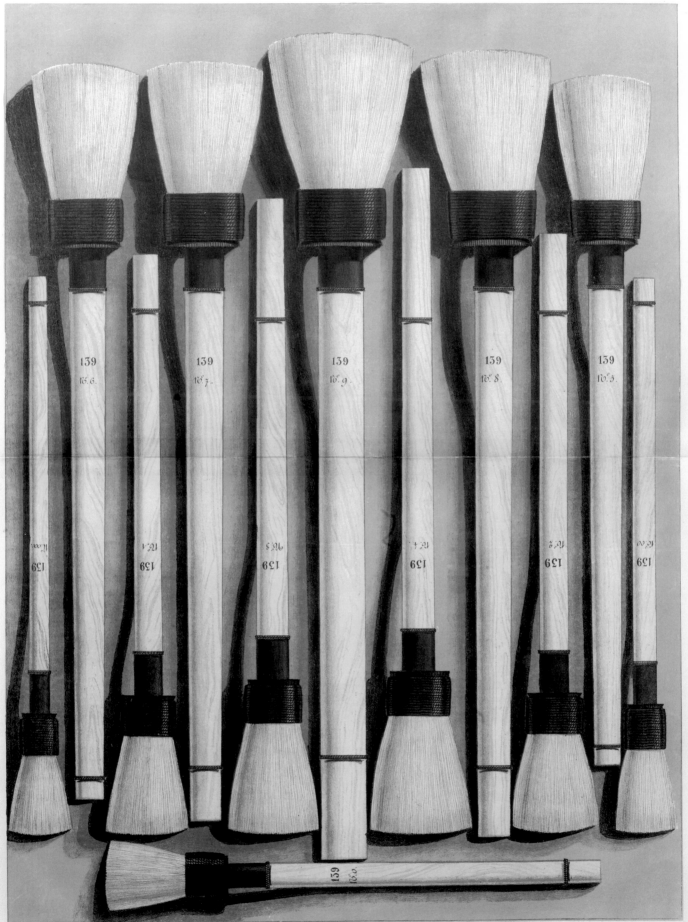

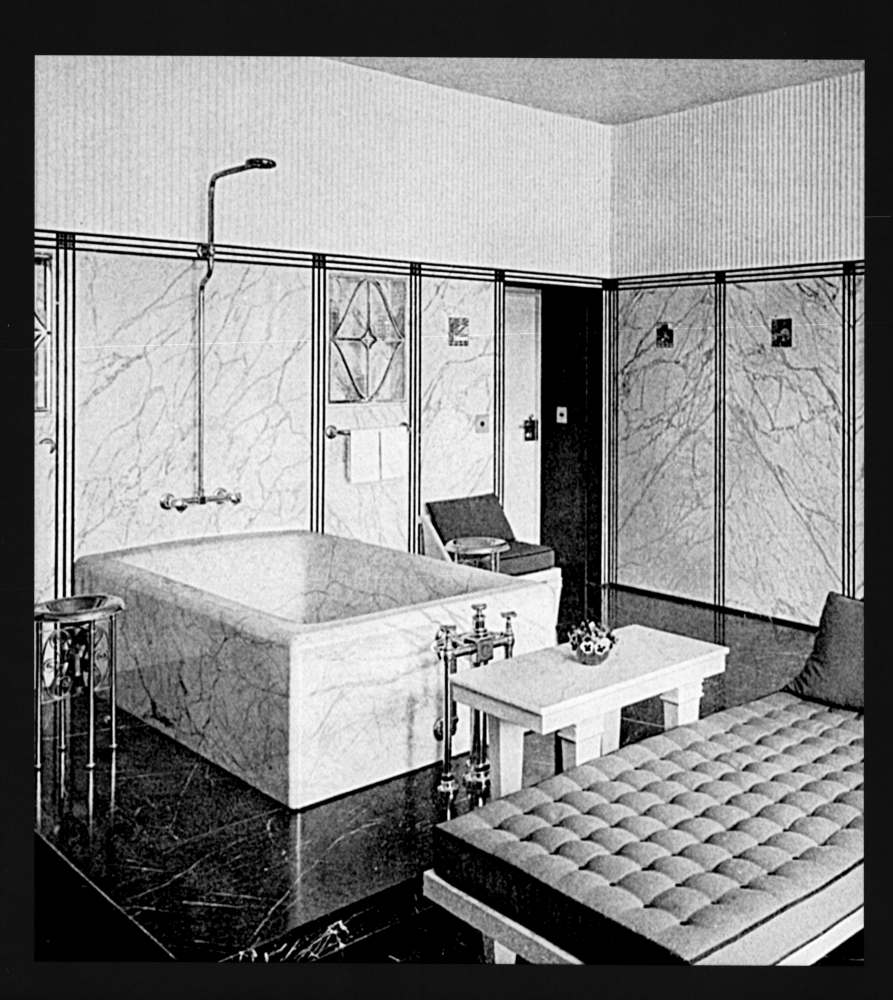

growing

For me, tending a garden, no matter how large or small,
has always been an essential part of my life.

I really caught the growing bug as a boy during the war when I did a lot of work on my parents' garden. We were all being urged to grow our own vegetables for the war effort and I found immense satisfaction in it. Growing is like designing: you start with a small seed, which then draws on everything around it – sun, water, minerals from the soil, and the care and attention you put into it as a gardener. The whole process is one of the most inspirational things in life and when you can eat your produce or admire a jug of flowers on your table, there is nothing more rewarding. Planting a garden is one of the best lessons in creativity that anyone can have. Vegetables require careful planning, preparation and nurturing, and if you are laying out a flower garden, you need to balance colour, form and texture, as well as trying to imagine what it is going to look like through the seasons, and in five years' time.

I find the sheer energy that occurs in my vegetable garden quite marvellous. This year a pumpkin grew from a compost heap on one side of the wall, found its way to the sunny top and grew big and heavy just hanging on the other side. It was one of the most charming and quirky things I have seen. I love the size and abundance of pumpkins, and in the autumn we put them all on a big table beside the front door.

One of the gardens I most admire is at Château de Villandry in France where the decorative qualities of vegetables have been used in a rather stunning way. A vast area is divided into squares by low box hedges and each one contains vegetables of contrasting colours – blue leeks, red cabbages, bright green carrot tops – all laid out in different geometric patterns. The effect is quite beautiful. For me, though, vegetable gardening has never been about the pursuit of perfection – I find a knobbly, misshapen squash equally as appealing as the symmetry of an artichoke head. Prehaps that is why I also enjoy old photographs and still life paintings of fruit and vegetables.

On the whole, I like rather modest gardens and prefer natural planting to formal. I think a wildflower meadow is probably better than any overcontrived modern garden and I like the way that grasses are being incorporated into contemporary schemes. Design is important, but when I go around the Chelsea Flower Show every year, I see a lot of designers being too clever. As far as I am concerned, the plants are the most important thing, not decking or architectural features, though if it is a big garden these can have their place. I have always liked the style of the English Arts and Crafts gardener Gertrude Jekyll, a classic plantswoman. Her drifts of colour and combinations of textures were intended to emulate nature rather than control it. The eighteenth-century landscape architect Capability Brown is another inspiration. His 'gardens' in the parklands of England's finest country houses used simple means, such as lakes and clumps of trees, to create natural landscapes that echoed the countryside. He brought grass meadows right up to the houses, separated from undulating lawns by invisible dropped walls called ha-has. The raised terrace at Barton Court serves the same purpose, so the garden flows out naturally into the water meadows, the edges disguised by the trees and planting. I think the thing I admire most about Brown is the confidence of his vision – his gardens were really great gestures to the future, as he knew he would never see his work in its full maturity. He called himself a 'placemaker', which to me is rather wonderful.

I try to keep everything natural in the walled garden at Barton Court. We plant vegetables and flowers together and I like to use simple materials for garden structures: tall cane pyramids for runner beans, fences made from hazel or willow cuttings, and paths built with bricks, pebbles or old railway sleepers. It is all part of an organic environment that is in tune with the growing process. There is also a cutting garden for flowers, as I love fresh flowers in the house and on my desk when I am working – roses and tulips are some of my favourites – and flowers are always an important part of the interior in my restaurants and hotels.

I gain a deep, elemental pleasure from my garden. Spring is my favourite season, when everything in the kitchen garden is just getting going, and what could be more beautiful than those lines of first seedlings popping up or the peas growing through the forest of hazel twigs? Later on, bringing in a basket of lettuce, peas and broad beans, with a punnet of strawberries or raspberries and a big bunch of sweetpeas, is pure joy. Inspiration doesn't come much better than this.

222

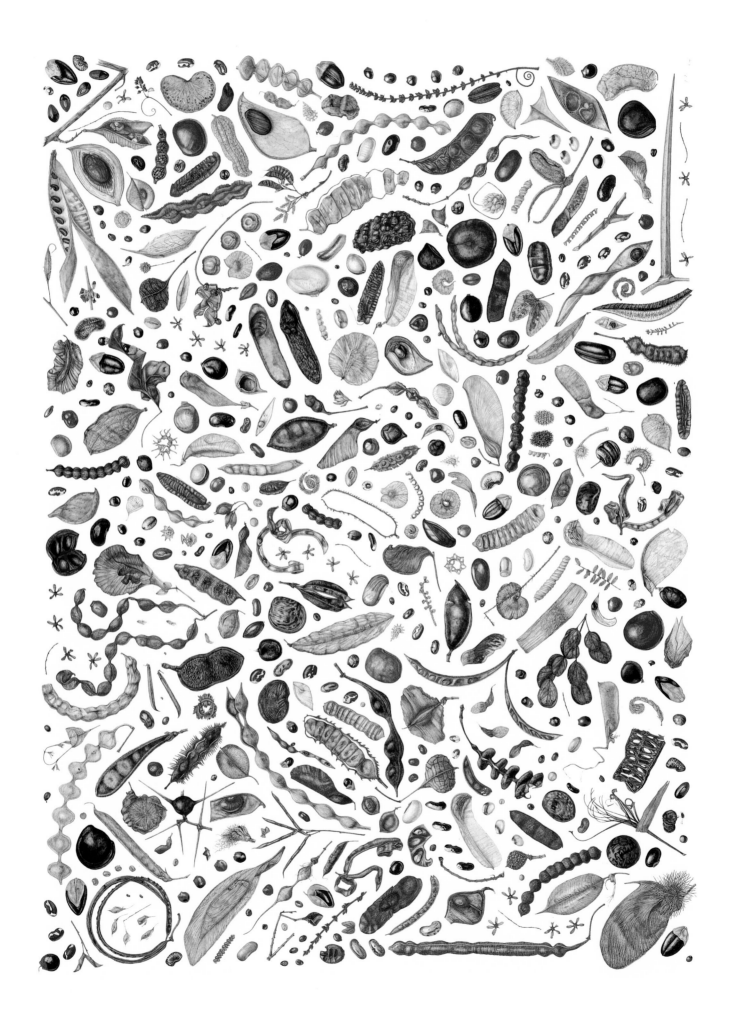

223

Verschiedene facconen von Pyramides, so von Taxis, Cypressen, und Seven können gesiegelt werden.

C.P.S.C.M.

M. Diesel inv. et del.

I.A. Corv. sculp.

Ier. Wolff excud. Aug. V.

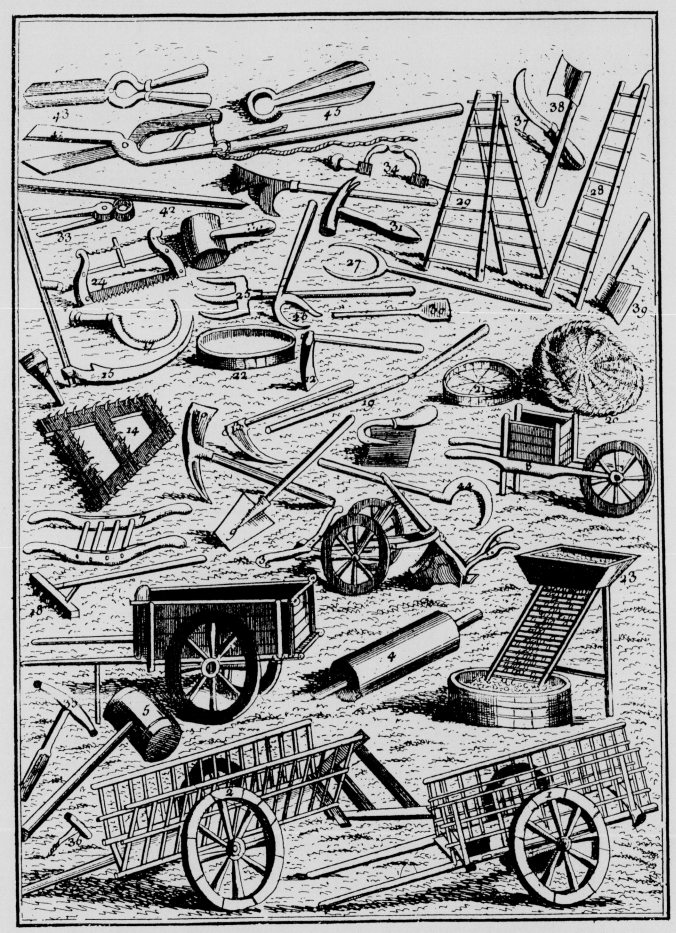

Non oderis Laboriosa opera, et rusticationem creatam ab altissimo.

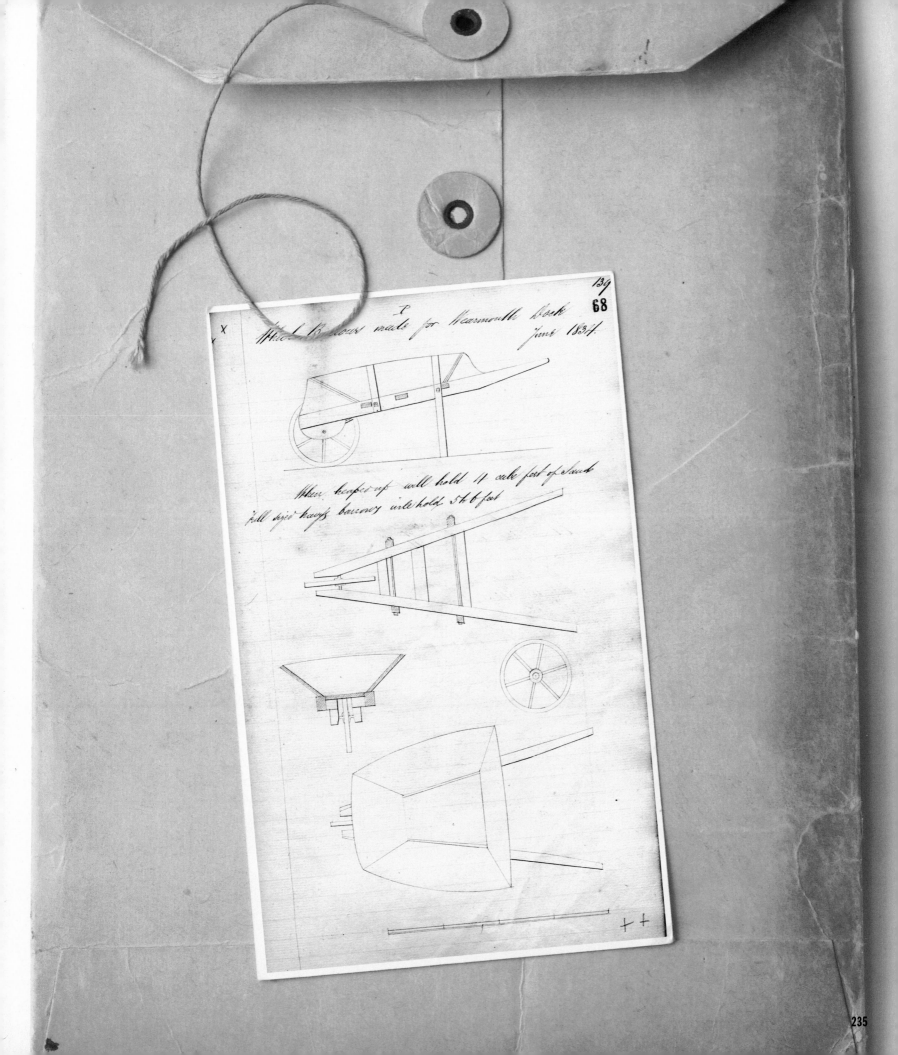

Wheel Barrows made for Wearmouth Dock
June 1834

When heaped up will hold 4 cube feet of Sand
Full sized wood barrows will hold 5 to 6 feet

FRITILLARIA
WALBERSWICK
1 9 1 5
C R M
M M M

passions

I live with design. Every moment of the day and quite a lot of the night I am thinking about the design of things or spaces.

With so many projects on the go, there is always an urgency to come up with solutions and directions. I find that even when I simply put things on a shelf or a table I am making decisions about how groups of objects look together. Eduardo Paolozzi, my tutor at design school, gave me a piece of advice that I have never forgotten: to go out and see as many things as possible, stock up your brain with images, and your imagination will have a resource to fall back on for many years.

I love museums for this reason, and also flea markets and junk shops. The museums I like best are rather fusty ones, such as the Science Museum or the Natural History Museum in London. There is one in Paris called the Quai Branly, which is wonderful because it is almost over-filled with indigenous ethnic art and artefacts, and you feel you might find inspiration for practically anything there. These places seem to have an authenticity that is sometimes missing from many contemporary museums where everything appears extremely precious. Rummaging around flea markets is another great spur to the imagination. I like seeing the incredible diversity of things people have made and spotting objects that, for me, connect to something else, which may be far removed from the objects' purpose. I learn from these things all the time.

When I discover something I like, it is generally because it has a sense of proportion, balance and individual character. I like plain, simple and useful things, such as old carpenters' tools that feel right in the hand, or a milk jug that has a certain modest elegance. I find that some of the most evocative objects are handmade – they have an ability to convey meaning and feeling that many manufactured pieces lack. That is not to say that factory-made objects are without merit; in my opinion, some of the best examples of modern design were created for mass production.

I often find that a reflection or a shadow is the inspiration for the shape of a product or part of the interior of a building, or, indeed, the building itself. I slightly fight against modern technology because, for many people, it doesn't allow them any time for contemplation. Taking a moment to notice small details – like the angle of sunshine coming into a room – is such an important part of our creative connection to the world. Simple things are inspiring, which is really what I want to say in this book. Don't, for example, forget about the plain wooden-beam structure of a barn when you are considering a new architectural scheme; traditional craftsmanship has a truthfulness to it that sometimes cannot be found elsewhere. It would be a shame if our towns and cities became entirely filled with hi-tech buildings, beautiful as they frequently are. An old stone bridge can be just as arresting as Norman Foster's latest piece of engineering and there should be a place for both. I feel very passionately about keeping a balance between the two.

I am also passionate in the belief that intelligent design should be accessible to all, both in our public spaces and in the things we put in our homes. I think I would have to agree with those who say that Habitat has been my greatest success, because it brought things that were well designed to the mass market at a price people could afford, and it made other retailers do the same. I am very keen to promote intelligent design. I have personally been greatly influenced by the artisans and designers of the English Arts and Crafts movement and the Bauhaus in 1920s Germany. With the Design Museum in London, which I founded, I have tried to provide a resource that informs people about contemporary design as well as celebrating it in all its forms. Throughout my career, I have worked with young designers, encouraging them in certain directions, adding ideas and experiencing the joy of seeing what they have achieved. My hope for the Design Museum is that it will serve as an inspiration and a springboard for everyone with an interest in design, and I would be delighted if a few people come away thinking 'I can do that'.

As you can see, design for me is hugely important. It has such a penetrating influence on how we live in the world that I feel very strongly that it should be at the centre of the cultural agenda. One of the great things about being a designer is that you have the opportunity to create something tangible that can potentially improve the quality of life, even in a small way. What I find most exciting about my work is the challenge of coming up with new solutions – my happiest moments are those with a 3B pencil and a pad of layout paper, especially when inspiration flows like adrenalin.

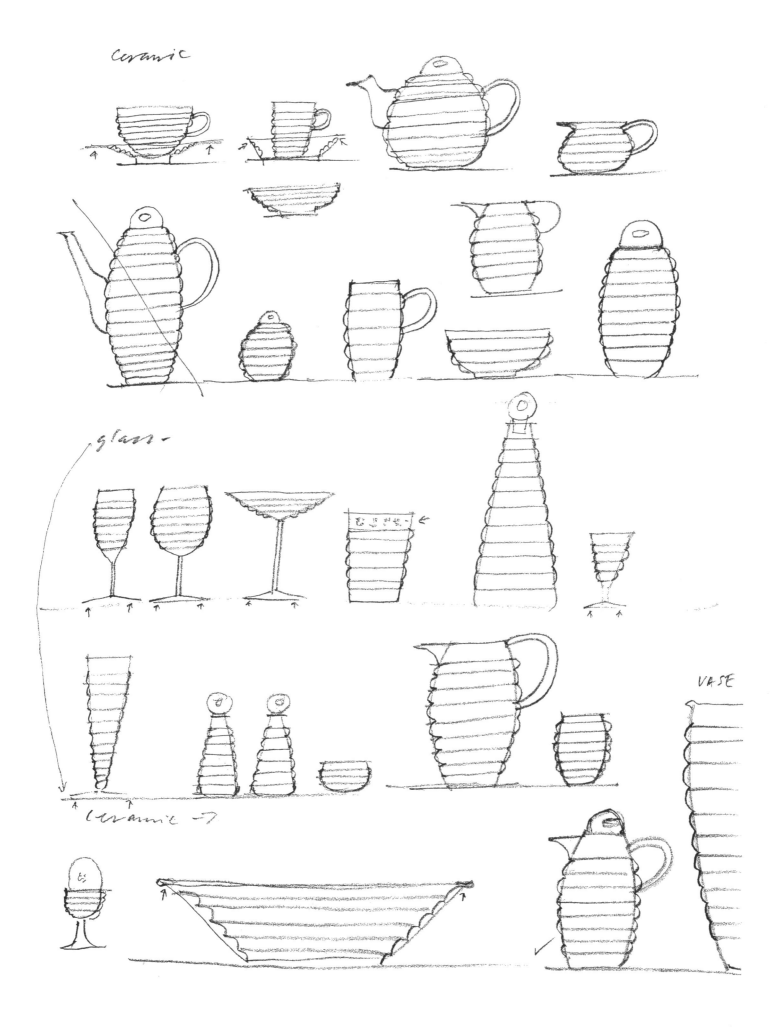

ceramic

glass

ceramic

VASE

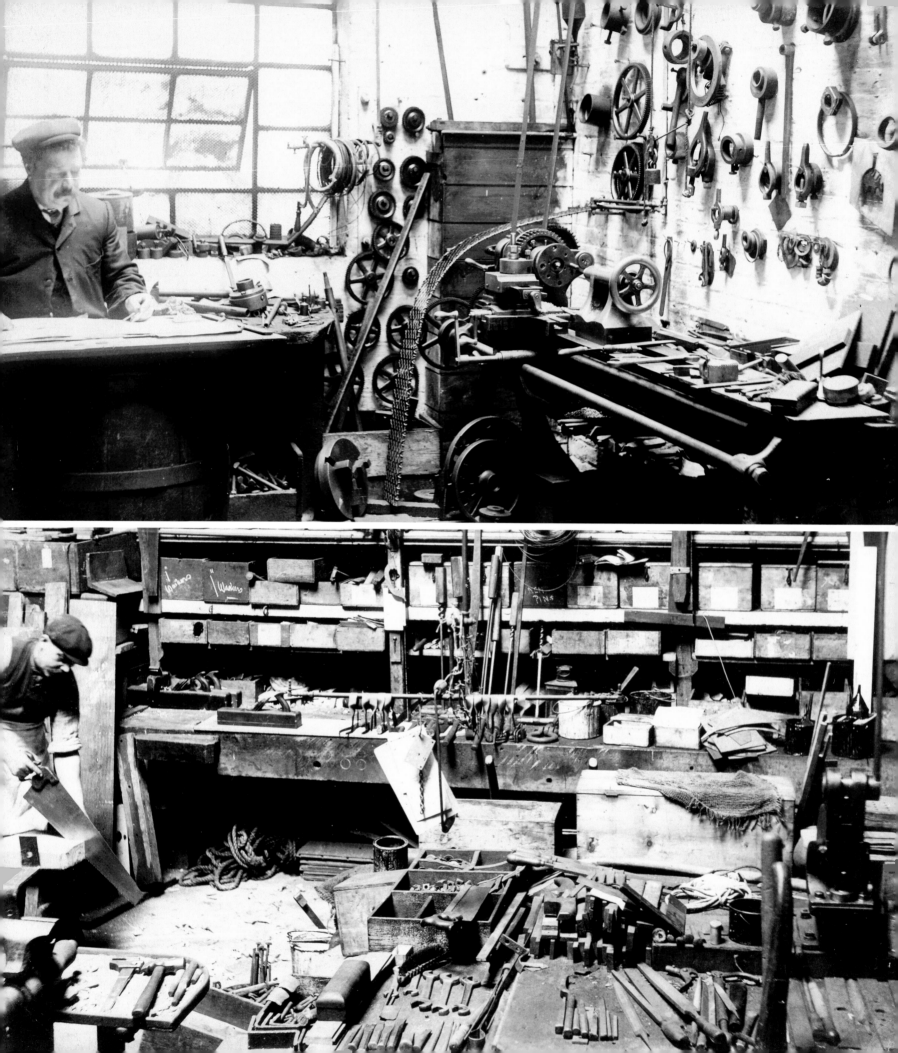

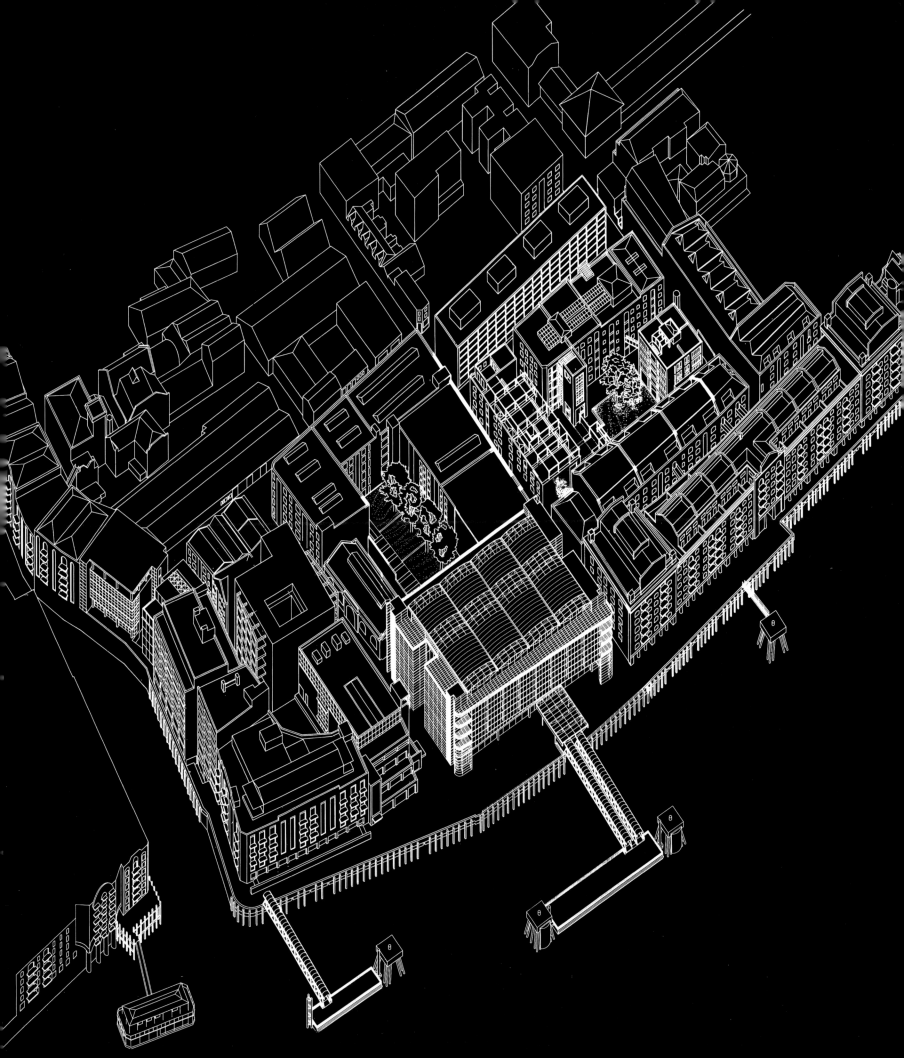

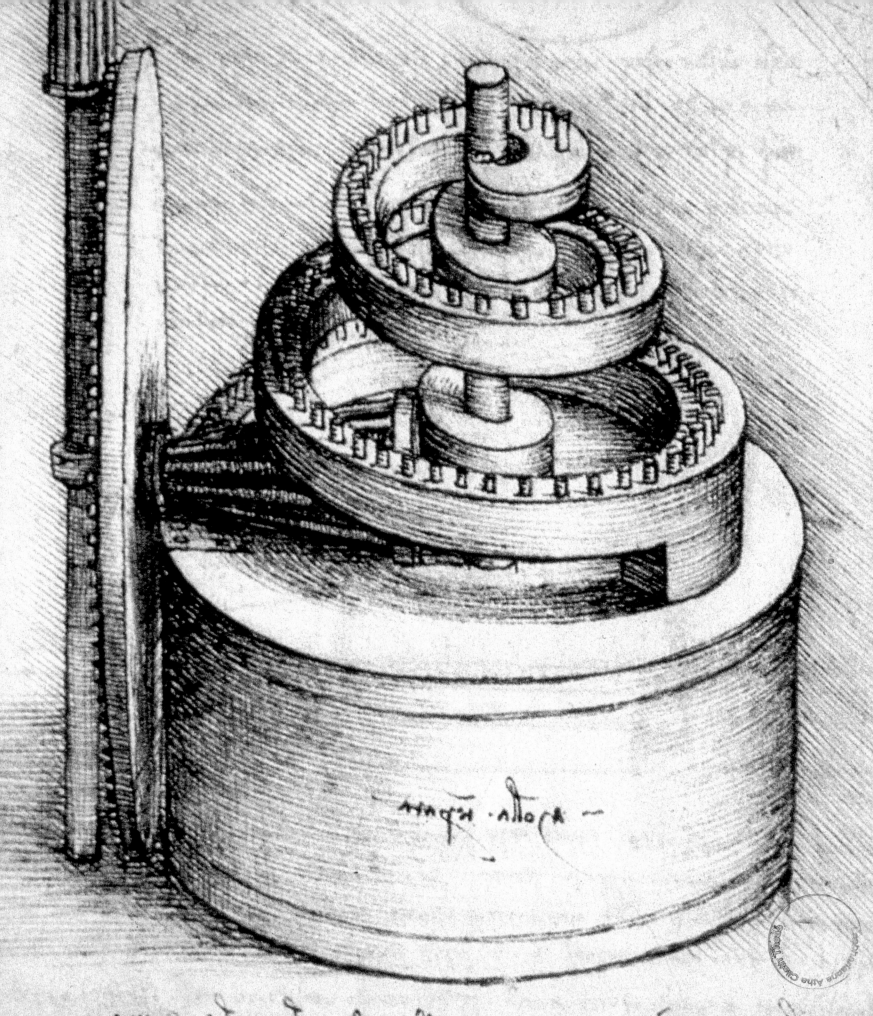

salui kqsu

Indoor Outdoor

Albany.

Loki dining

Mad Axe 8

Hudson side & Arm.

Avro

Portobello.

Loki rectangular.

Haven.

interlock shelving

Luka

Moo-stool

Bradley

MONDRIAN

Nola chair

overhang single & double

CONE

Chest of drawers Niagara

Phy

Mocha chair & table.

Turo

pythagoras - Sycamore & Ash.

Nila

Roller table high.

Hed Bridge & tunnel.

York

Cog

Plaza

Oskar

Zinc Turo.

Woodframe armchair & sofa

Shad Thames wedge

Berlin lamp.

Acorn

Oslo

Rembrandt

Zinc cube.

Normandie II

Star

Roller table low.

Radius coffee table

Normandie II side board

concord.

Single version 1 x 60 x 60

Tribune square & round -

11 AT DOOR bedside.

New Modular

273

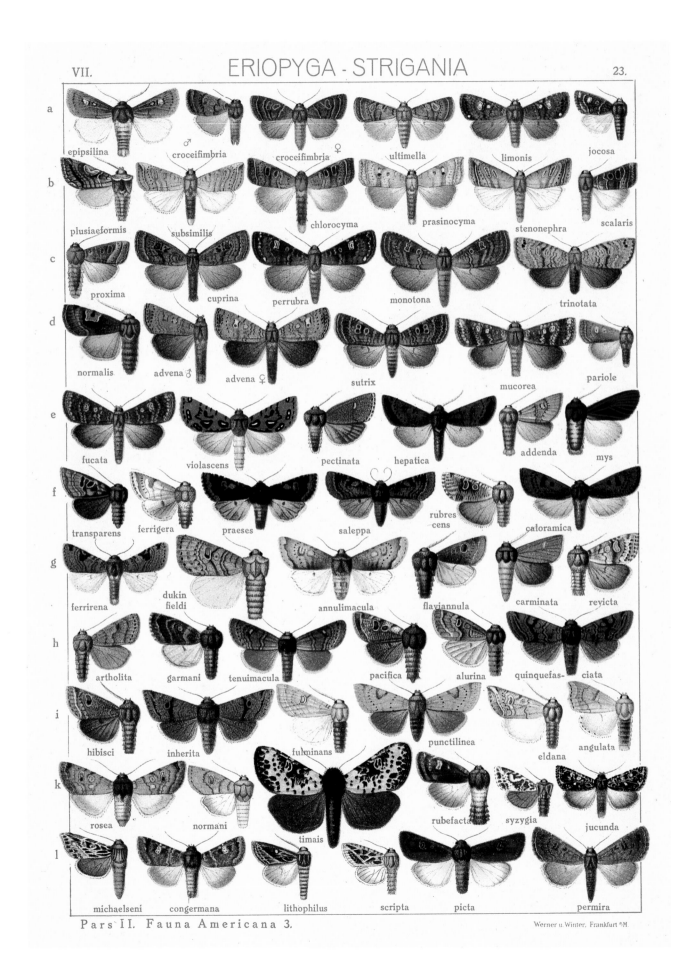

epipsilina   croceifimbria ♂   croceifimbria ♀   ultimella   limonis   jocosa

plusiaeformis   subsimilis   chlorocyma   prasinocyma   stenonephra   scalaris

proxima   cuprina   perrubra   monotona   trinotata

normalis   advena ♂   advena ♀   sutrix   mucorea   pariole

fucata   violascens   pectinata   hepatica   addenda   mys

transparens   ferrigera   praeses   saleppa   rubrescens   caloramica

ferrirena   dukinfieldi   annulimacula   flaviannula   carminata   revicta

artholita   garmani   tenuimacula   pacifica   alurina   quinquefas- ciata

hibisci   inherita   fulminans   punctilinea   eldana   angulata

rosea   normani   timais   rubefacta   syzygia   jucunda

michaelseni   congermana   lithophilus   scripta   picta   permira

Pars II. Fauna Americana 3.

Werner u. Winter, Frankfurt ª M.

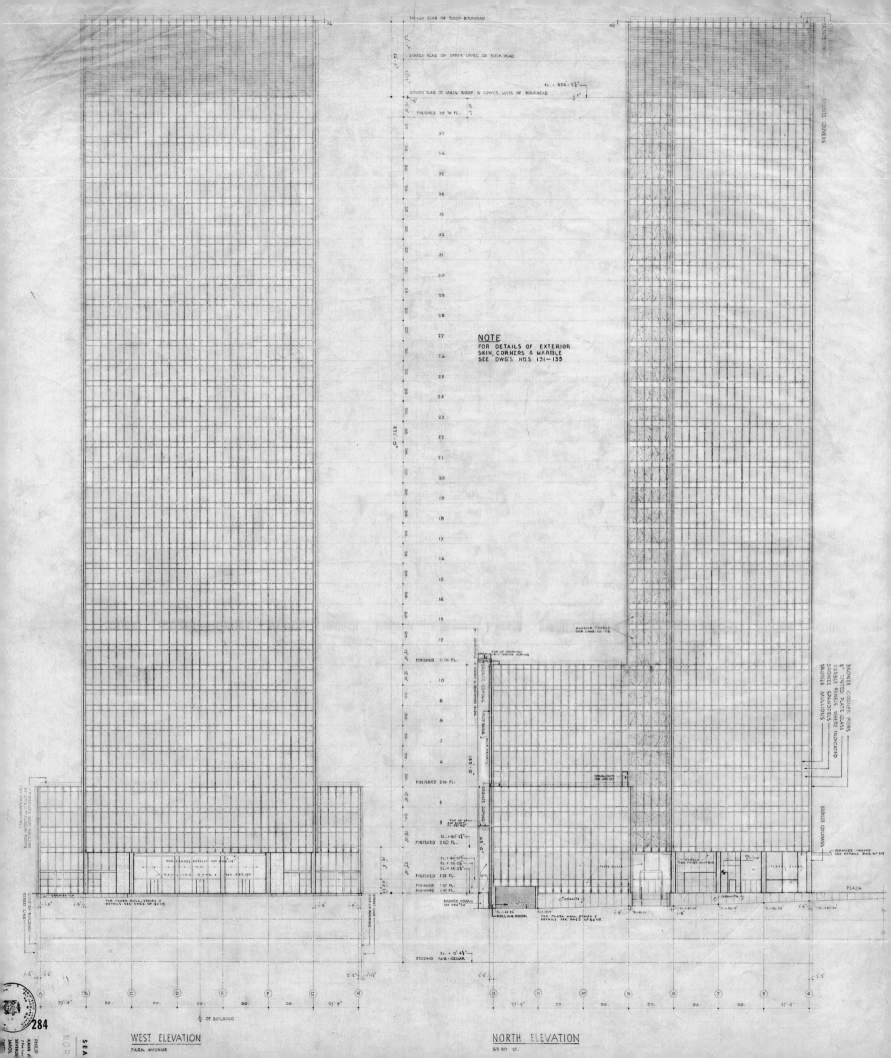

NOTE
FOR DETAILS OF EXTERIOR
SKIN, CORNERS & MARBLE
SEE DWG'S NO.S 131-135

WEST ELEVATION
PARK AVENUE

NORTH ELEVATION
53 RD ST.

Page 4 I am very fond of this little watercolour painting of me done by my son Tom a couple of years ago. It stands on the mantelpiece above one of the two fireplaces in the living room.

Page 6 As you approach Barton Court along the driveway, you glimpse the east side through the horse chestnuts. The kitchen, my office and Vicki's office above mine are all located here. We have evidence of its former incarnation as a fine country residence in a leatherbound game book we received from the previous owners. In it, it lists the results of a day's shooting on 19 November 1902, six guns bagged 170 pheasants, 8 ducks, 25 hares and 13 rabbits – they must have made several splendid dinners.

Page 8 This was once the front door, but I moved the main entrance to the other side when I bought the house. It is now a wonderfully tranquil place to sit in the sun and enjoy the southerly view along the terrace, particularly in the late afternoon.

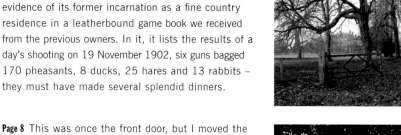

Page 10 This French château-style birdcage has been with me for as long as I can remember. When my daughter Sophie was little it was filled with canaries, but I don't really like having caged birds, so now it stands empty, silhouetted in one of the windows in the living room.

the house

Pages 12–13 Taken by our gardener Jon Chidsey during the winter of 2007, this magical photograph shows the southern aspect of the house. From this viewpoint you can see the raised terrace and the vista I created from the old front door down to the river. The enormous terracotta Greek urn is one of several that I bought many years ago.

Page 14 On the river meadow in front of Barton Court, four life-size deer by the British sculptor Nick Munro look up from their peaceful grazing to contemplate the house. When they arrived in 1975, they stood on the other side of the field, but a tree later fell on several of them, so the herd have regrouped near the topiary.

Page 15 The upstairs windows provide good views of the surrounding gardens and farmland: to the south you can see beyond the raised terrace to a sculptural wooden gazebo by the British designer Thomas Heatherwick and behind that the river, though the trees are considerably bigger than this now; on the north side, you get a splendid overview of the walled garden and conservatories.

Page 16 In the 1940s and 1950s, Barton Court was home to a boys' preparatory school. This wonderful picture shows the pupils of Purton Stoke School lined up outside for their end-of-term photograph. I see that there were ten staff in all, including the headmaster and matron and 75 pupils. When the school's tenancy ended, the house was abandoned and became derelict, which was how I found it in 1971. People who saw it then said, 'How on earth can you live in this place? It's got the smell of smacked bottoms.'

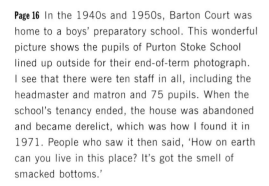

Page 17 This picture of me in front of the house was taken shortly after we bought it and the builders moved in. You can see the dreary gravel driveway that came right up to the front door, and behind me, one of the broken windows is still boarded up.

Page 18 When we bought the house, there was a servants' staircase running parallel to this one, but we removed it and used the space for a series of bathrooms and lavatories. This picture rather reminds me of Kettle's Yard in Cambridge (see page 63), where every ledge has a collection displayed on it.

Page 19 This horse, which I have had for many years, came from a shop that sold saddlery. Its purpose was for trying out new saddles, which would be put on its back so you could jump up and see if the saddle was the right size. It is made of wood, which was originally covered with pony skin. I bought it from David Hicks's shop in Chesham Place, London, and I still can't quite believe that he was happy to let it go.

Page 20 This is the first-floor landing outside our bedroom. The sofa on the left is my interpretation of the classic Lutyens garden bench and above it hangs an Indian cloth picture. I have never been keen on wall-to-wall carpet in my homes: I prefer to show beautiful old floorboards where they exist with lots of rugs or Indian dhurries.

Page 21 I designed this six-tier console to fit into the beautiful first-floor window so that I could display some of my collection of bottles and glassware. Here the light shines through them and they can be seen at their best. The simple display cabinet on the right, showcasing a variety of my favourite objects, was also made here some time ago by my furniture company, Benchmark.

Page 22 This magnificent collection of 20 Bugatti pedal cars, all beautifully restored and resprayed, came from a man who was the director of Ford France. He had been collecting them for years, but no longer had room for them. I soon realised, though, that I had the same problem – until I hit upon a solution: to hang them all on the wall of the ground-floor corridor like a collection of moths or beetles.

Page 23 This picture was taken a year ago for The Conran Shop Christmas catalogue – just so you know that I don't ride up and down the corridors here with little girls every day.

Page 24 Like a theatre for the automobiles, this is the interior of the Le Marbeuf garage for Citroën Cars in Paris, designed by Albert Laprade and L. E. Bazin in 1929. I am amused to compare it to the recently opened C43 building on the Champs Elysées, which has been designed by the French architect Manuelle Gautrand, and which showcases rather different, more modern vehicles.

Page 25 I love this photograph of a pedal-car race at a garden party in 1933. I like the design of the cars and the fact that the grown-ups seem to be taking it all so seriously. It would be fun to do the same here on the lawn at Barton Court, but I have 20 cars and only 11 grandchildren so far.

Page 26 Launched at the Tokyo Motor Show in 2003, the 'Cube 3' concept car was a joint venture between Conran & Partners and the Japanese car manufacturer Nissan. Our approach was to view the car as a movable environment: a kind of room on wheels and a place in which one could feel at home. The initial limited edition sold out immediately.

Page 27 When I first saw it, I thought that Wells Coates's Lancia (top) was one of the most beautiful cars I had ever seen. Coates was a Canadian modernist designer and architect, and this would surely have been the type of car he would have designed for himself. I love open-top cars and I have a Porsche at the moment. The first time I went to France with my friend Michael Wickham, we travelled in his Lagonda, but it was not as old as this one (bottom).

Page 28 In 1953 I took a now legendary trip through France with Michael Wickham (see pages 54–55), then a Condé Nast photographer, his wife Cynthia and Patricia Lyttelton, who was a freelance illustrator for *House & Garden*. We spent the whole trip drawing and painting, and Michael did this sketch of me in his notebook looking somewhat unkempt, at Bonneval near Chartres.

living

Page 30 This picture of the living room, taken by Tony Snowdon in 1982, looks towards what once would have been the front of the house. I retained the original stone floor tiles but removed the walls on either side, making the three rooms into one enormous open space. The large globe was a 21st birthday present from my mother.

Page 31 Here is the same room 20 years later. I found the 1930s metal table, broken and without a top, in Isle-sur-la-Sorgue in the south of France, and for a while it was in my London apartment. I admire the workmanship and I gave it a glass top to emphasize the tracery of the frame. It is one of my favourite things. The old vaulting buck came from a shop in Hungerford, the source of quite a lot of my best objects over the years. I thought it was like a piece of sculpture, but in fact it has inspired one of my Benchmark designers to make a bench seat like it.

Pages 32–33 Running along the entire front of the house, the living room at Barton Court, with its tall windows and pale colours, has always been the perfect place for me to display my various collections and try out new furniture I have designed. This picture was taken in the 1980s and the brown sofa later turned up in the Habitat catalogue; the coffee table was a design that we sold in The Conran Shop.

Page 34 When Caroline and I bought our house in Provence, this room was a barn so we had to convert it. I left the timbers exposed and put in the new stone fireplace, on which is a collection of locally found things that I liked the look of. We put throws over the white Habitat sofas because of the endless comings and goings of children in damp swimming costumes. The house was called Brunellys and was sold in 2006.

Page 35 You may think, as you look at these pictures of the house taken over the years, that you keep seeing the same pieces of furniture and art. The truth is that you do. These are things I have loved all my life and that still give me pleasure. What more can you say of a thing that someone has made?

Page 36 This is another photograph of the living room from the series taken by Tony Snowdon in 1982. Since then it has evolved quite a lot; the TV has moved to the kitchen and the metal campaign chair has gone. The Arco floor lamp is still there, however – I rarely get rid of anything, it just moves about.

Page 37 This is the same view now. With this sofa I was trying to design a contemporary alternative to the Chesterfield and Burnham sofas that we sold so many of in The Conran Shop over the years.

Page 38 This is what I call my private museum; it consists of things I have liked and collected, and they remain a constant source of inspiration to me. I add new things from time to time. I designed the unit seating for The Conran Shop and also the chess board because I like playing chess very much. The cushion is a patchwork of antique Japanese kimono silk that I bought in New York.

Page 39 The 'Summa' storage range was designed in 1963 and made in our furniture factory at Thetford in Norfolk (see page 111). The series of modular components included doors, shelves and tall or shallow trays-cum-drawers; the three levels fitted together with a series of little steel pegs. It amuses me to notice in this display one or two objects I still have at home, including the little brown phrenology head and, even then, the cigar boxes.

Page 40 I wanted to put something on the riverfront outside the Design Museum in London, so I asked Eduardo Paolozzi. He decided to do something about 'intelligence made visible', inspired by a dissected model of Thomas Watt's in the Science Museum. On the base we used a quotation from da Vinci: 'Though human genius in its various inventions with various instruments may answer the same end, it will never find an invention more beautiful or more simple or more direct than nature, because in her inventions nothing is lacking and nothing is superfluous.'

Page 41 We called the simple seamless shelves that run the whole width of one end of the Barton Court living room 'bull nose' shelves, and we used them on a number of commissions throughout the 1970s, including our own offices in Neal Street, London. I think they were designed by my dear friend and colleague Oliver Gregory and I still cannot imagine a better design. In this picture there are two prints by Richard Smith (see page 147) and several heads by Eduardo Paolozzi, including the maquette he made for the sculpture outside the Design Museum.

Page 42 This portrait was done by Eduardo Paolozzi in the 1950s. Eduardo taught me textile design in 1949 at the Central School of Arts and Crafts in London and we became friends for life. His work embraced graphics and painting as well as sculpture; his most celebrated work is probably the figure of Sir Isaac Newton in the forecourt of the British Library and the decoration of London's Tottenham Court Road Underground station.

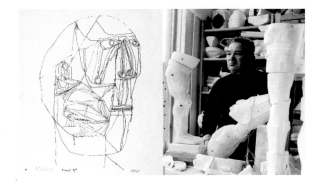

Page 43 When Eduardo and I first met, he had just returned from Paris and was beginning to make his name as a sculptor. He was extremely rugged, extremely poor (like the rest of us) and oozed creativity. Everything he touched with his large podgy hands turned into a wonderful organic object and every mark he made on paper was beautiful to my eyes. I commissioned him whenever I could; in 1973 he produced a limited edition print for the opening of the Habitat store in King's Road, London.

Page 44 I find this picture strangely mesmerizing – perhaps it is the colour or the smooth creamy surface broken by a blemish like that on a piece of pottery. In fact, it is the 800m (half-a-mile-) wide Victoria Crater on Mars. You can see the pattern of crumbling rocks and erosion around the edge and, in the centre, a little pattern of sand dunes. In 2004 the Rover Opportunity, a Mars exploration vehicle, drove 9km (5 miles) to reach the crater and you can just see it parked at roughly the ten o'clock position on the rim.

Page 46 A log fire is practically one of the only joys of the seemingly endless English winter, though I do love rugging up and going for a walk around the garden on a crisp frosty morning. Consequently, log baskets – the bigger the better – have been constant friends. This one in the kitchen was made for us in willow by the British basket maker Jenny Crisp and stands about 1.5m (5ft) high.

Page 48 The director of Benchmark, Sean Sutcliffe trained as a designer and cabinetmaker and came to see me in 1984 when he was just out of college. At first we had a small prototype workshop; I did sketches of pieces and he made them work. For ten years we worked together each Saturday, on small products for The Conran Shop or Habitat, or on pieces for my house in Provence. As time went on, we began to get work for outside clients and built up the team. Since then – starting with Bibendum – they have worked on each of my restaurants.

Page 50 These lacquered wood shelves hold more of my treasures. At the top is a sleek racing car given to me by Norman Foster; on the second shelf the small winged lion is an insurance company's sign that was on the front of the house here, and to the right is a Japanese basket, a little figure by Eduardo Paolozzi, and a figure by the British sculptor Lynn Chadwick; on the next shelf is a small red painting by the British painter Stephen Buckley, a wooden hat mould and a cone of sugar; the framed stamp collage on the bottom shelf was done by Vicki's son Toby.

Page 52 This Thomas Heatherwick glass chair was another gift from my daughter Sophie. Although I like most of Tom's work, this piece is part of a trend that I find rather worrying: designers are producing pieces of furniture as artworks, which then fetch huge sums of money in the art world. I am very much against this. I like this chair as a sculpture, but you certainly can't sit with any degree of comfort on it.

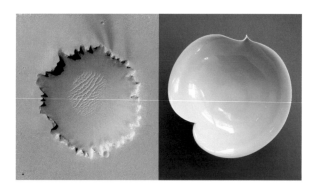

Page 45 This beautiful porcelain bowl is by the Japanese potter Kawase Shinobu, whose work I had seen and admired. When I mentioned this to my friend David Queensberry, he managed to contact a friend in Japan who knew him and collected his work. She had him make this piece especially for me. I find it truly inspirational.

Page 47 Although it is the diseased growth from an oak tree, the burr is prized for its texture and its ultimately imperfect qualities. One of the Benchmark team has sculpted this piece, discarded from a trunk, into a bowl. I am always looking for ways to recycle the waste material from our factory – this is one of the more imaginative.

Page 49 In 1907 the Romanian sculptor Constantin Brancusi adopted a new approach to his work by carving his materials directly, without using clay models or maquettes first. I love the totemlike presence of his wooden columns and the fact that he often used reclaimed house timber. Some, like 'King of Kings' in this picture, look a bit mysterious, like some sort of religious idol. I think that museum recreations of artists' studios are very important; Brancusi's adjoins the Centre Pompidou in Paris.

Page 51 I love ammonites. I have always been interested in natural forms – eggs, flowers, trees, butterflies. All are the essence of inspiration. On the ledge above the living-room fireplace I have put an ammonite beside a bowl that my daughter Sophie gave me for my seventieth birthday; it was made by the New York jewellery designer Ted Muehling.

Page 53 This chair, given to me by my parents, came from West Woodhay House, my grandmother's family home, which was just near here. I have transformed it from an old fashioned-looking piece of furniture by recovering it in orangey-red velvet, so that it now looks modern.

Page 54 Accompanied by an extraordinary editorial attacking contemporary furniture, *House & Garden* ran this photograph by Michael Wickham in its 1954 annual review of the latest designs. It included a yellow-and-black upholstered chair by Robin Day, and my chair in two colours of tweed with metal legs.

Page 55 Not only a photographer, Michael Wickham was also something of a craftsman. He both designed and built these room sets for *House & Garden* and, in this one, he used solely my furniture, except the coffee table, to demonstrate 'a north-facing dining room with three glowing colours: persimmon, nasturtium and cherry'. Michael was a dear friend and a true inspiration. In later years, he worked in the studio at Barton Court where he had a great influence on many young designers.

Page 56 These small ads in a 1954 edition of *House & Garden* show some of the furniture that I was selling from a tiny showroom in a basement in Piccadilly Arcade in London. A lot of the furniture I made was metal-framed because I knew how to weld and I liked the skinny-linear quality. One particular success was the three-legged cone-shaped planter, which still crops up from time to time. Ray Williams took the photographs (see pages 60–61).

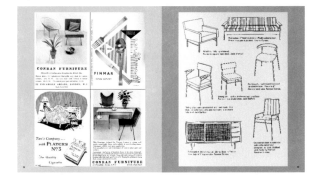

Page 57 In 1966 some of my furniture designs appeared in a book called *British Furniture Through the Ages*. In his introduction Robert Keith Middlemas wrote, 'The best modern design is probably to be found, not in domestic furniture, but in contract work for public buildings. Independent designers and architects can establish styles which the market cannot accept... Once the contract designs have proved their worth, they influence the retail market, but it is still too early to suggest that British design is as influential as its merits deserve.'

Page 58 This was the public library in Luton, Bedfordshire that I designed in 1962. I used my signature shelving in square metal tube with insets in African walnut. The 'Abacus' seating was part of our range, but the light fitting was by a firm that I worked for at the time called Troughton & Young. I have no idea if anything survived, but I still like the way it looks.

Page 59 One of the first potteries to produce modern tableware in the UK was Midwinter. Roy Midwinter's 1953 'Stylecraft' range was influenced by the natural forms he had seen in America and was a huge success. I created a number of patterns for the company (see page 279) and, in 1956, I was also asked to design its showroom in Stoke-on-Trent. I divided the rectangular space into domestic-size bays using timber-slatted dividers; my signature shelving had silk-screened panels with some of my patterns. The scheme was basically black and white.

Pages 60–61 The photographer Ray Williams lived below us at 11 Regent's Park Terrace, London, and he kindly sent me these contact sheets recently. He took them in 1952 to promote some of my furniture pieces and also took some still-life pictures of kitchen objects, which I used as panels in The Soup Kitchen and The Orrery restaurant in King's Road. We recently remade the cone chair for The Conran Shop (see back cover).

Page 62 This fascinating page from the archives of Willows of Lancaster, dated 1798, shows a sketch of a Windsor chair for the purposes of calculating the costs of manufacture. Using 1.3m (4ft 3in) of elm in the seat, and 1.5m (5ft) of cherry tree in the legs, back, elbows and spindles, the cost – including construction – came to 9 shillings.

Page 63 This is the first-floor sitting room of Kettle's Yard in Cambridge, the home until 1973 of the collector Jim Ede. It is part private home, part art gallery, part music space. I like the house for its collection of 1920s British art, its multitude of interesting chairs and its deeply personal arrangements of contemplative objects. In this photograph the marble sculpture of a small dog on the top step is by the early twentieth-century French sculptor Henri Gaudier-Brzeska.

Page 64 In 1965 we worked with Gillette on its factory complex at Isleworth in Greater London, designing interiors for bars, games rooms and billiard rooms, as well as a complete catering facility and this theatre. The ceiling was a series of cantilevered fins that concealed lighting and air conditioning, and the chairs were by Charles Eames.

Page 65 To most furniture designers, the American couple Charles and Ray Eames are considered the most important designers of the twentieth century. This range of moulded-plywood furniture is from the mid-1940s; the inspiration for the chairs is said to come from American vernacular forms such as tractor seats and jump seats in cars. For the first time, the furniture of the Eameses, Eero Saarinen and George Nelson is having a rather late flowering in America, having previously been available only through contract-only showrooms.

Page 66 Designed in 1934 by the British furniture maker Gerald Summers, this elegant bentwood chair was the first to be made from a single sheet of plywood. It was made by a company called Makers of Simple Furniture Ltd in London and its production, which employed steam to mould the plywood, involved no assembly process whatsoever – a feature that pleases me greatly – and I am puzzled as to why a great many of them were not produced.

Page 67 The great German modernist Ludwig Mies van der Rohe was also experimenting with this furniture-making technique in the early 1930s. This coloured pencil sketch shows his design for a split bentwood armchair. It reminds me of another of his chairs, made from chrome and canework, which we introduced into Habitat, and which we had in both our design offices and at home for many years. It was exceedingly comfortable, but you tended to knock your leg on the protruding front curve as you stood up.

Page 68 (Above) This 1960s picture shows our 'Abacus' unit seating, which was very popular at that time, particularly for universities. It is very pleasing to see beside it the SK4 record player, which was designed for Braun by Dieter Rams and Hans Gugelot, and 'House of Cards' by Charles Eames, on the table. **(Below)** Made in our factory in Thetford in the 1960s, this chair and day bed were probably inspired by the Italian furniture designer Vico Magistretti, whose chair we used to make under licence. In fact, we are now reintroducing the chair into The Conran Shop.

Page 69 (Above) When we moved the wood- and metalworking facilities to Thetford in Norfolk, we also acquired an old maltings building and began to produce upholstery there. I am glad to report that it is now owned by the furniture company SCP. **(Below)** Producing furniture that was part wood or metal frame and part upholstery made it more domestic, I think, probably because of the colour and texture from the fabric. This box with a sliding top was quite successful – you could put drinks inside it and it became a rather more acceptable bar.

Pages 70–71 The top-floor living area in our Shad Thames apartment in London is focused on the Danish stove, which in winter gives out a huge amount of heat. I designed the two sofas – not very comfortable, I'm afraid – and the zinc-topped coffee table. Regrettably, the lovely rug from India is not one of my designs, nor is the leather chair – my favourite – which was designed by the Finn Yrjö Kukkapuro. On the far wall is a tribal shield, made from rhinoceros hide by the Oroma people of southern Ethiopia.

Page 72 I was only 16 when I began a three-year course in Textile Design at the Central School of Arts and Crafts in London and it made a very strong impression on me. The course was run by a lady called Dora Batty. I learnt screen printing and discovered the Bauhaus and the Arts and Crafts movement, and my whole attitude to life was really formed in those couple of years. I felt, and still feel, very strongly that good design should be something that is available to the entire community. This was the Textiles class in 1955.

Page 73 This was the Conran Interior Design studio on the first floor of a building in Hanway Place, London, which we converted from a bomb-damaged Jewish charitable school in 1961. Here we developed one of the first multidisciplinary design studios in the UK, producing interiors, products, furniture, exhibitions and graphic design work, both for ourselves and for external clients. This is how it looked when Stafford Cliff joined us as a designer.

Page 74 I have placed enormous insects like this one, along the top shelf in my library. They came from a French university and were used for teaching purposes – you can remove layers to reveal the guts of beetles, caterpillars, and so forth. I got them as a group from a shop in the Fulham Road, London.

Page 75 This is my library at Barton Court. The shelves are supported by hidden brackets sunk into the walls and are interspersed with stained-timber light boxes that support and divide the books, and also help to illuminate the room. The portraits on the top shelf, one of which is by Reynolds, are of my grandmother's family.

Page 76 I vividly remember the look and feel of London's Covent Garden when I moved the design office there in 1970: the streets crowded every morning with trucks loading and unloading vegetables and fruit; the open-fronted warehouses in Neal Street and Shelton Street, full of boxes and bags of produce; and the joy of wandering through Floral Hall and Jubilee Hall, seeing the colourful products and even more colourful characters.

Page 77 On 5 January 1971 we relaunched the Design Group in a converted fruit and vegetable warehouse on Neal Street in Covent Garden. We celebrated the fact by mailing out this poster illustrated by Tony Meuwissen, much to the horror of our ex-partners, the Ryman brothers, who didn't expect us to bounce back so quickly after the demerger. You can see them looking in the window near the plant pot.

Page 78 This Eric Ravilious drawing is from a 1938 book called *High Street*. 'This type of restaurant is one for which London has been famous for a long time', reads the accompanying text, going on to explain that 'Grilling is done in public so that the customers can choose their piece of meat before it is cooked and say when it is sufficiently done.' Finally, it claims, somewhat mystifyingly, that 'Chefs generally have small feet and wear rather pointed shoes; and they very often seem to have a drooping moustache.'

cooking

Pages 80–81 This is the kitchen at Barton Court. It is part of a Victorian addition to the original house and was formerly a snooker room. Later, when Barton Court was a school, it was used as the assembly room. The large extract canopy made an ideal place to store all the pots and pans that most people seem to want to hide away. When Caroline was here it was always full of the smells of cooking as she tested recipes for the various recipe books and food articles she wrote. The children always seemed to gravitate towards this room.

Page 82 Taken in the 1980s, this picture shows all the elements I believe are important for a successful family kitchen: cooking within sight and sound of the eating area, practical but comfortable chairs, a generous easy-to-clean table, plenty of light, plain neutral walls and floors, and a glowing open fire.

Page 83 One of my favourite times of any day is lunchtime and I love the big relaxed lunches we have, usually at the weekends, when artists, designers, business friends or children might come to stay. On this occasion, in May 2004, we were having *bœuf à la mode*, which Jeremy Lee (far end of the table), head chef at the Blue Print Café in London, had just cooked for an *Observer Food Magazine* photo shoot.

Pages 84–85 Now that the family have all grown up, the room has taken on a calmer air, but there is still just as much cooking going on, as Vicki creates recipes for photo shoots or we cook together for friends. The children – now with my grandchildren in tow – still gather here for riotous birthday parties or festive celebrations.

Page 86 This page of immaculately drawn artefacts comes from the portfolio of the nineteenth-century Swedish archaeologists Bror Emil Hildebrand and Hans Hildebrand. The beautiful stone spearheads illustrate perfectly the (intelligent) designer's dictum that form follows function.

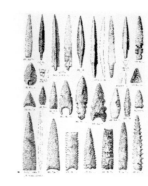

Page 87 A small blade for scoring pork, tweezers for pin-boning fish, a truffle slice, and numerous knives and knife sharpeners – these are the tools of trade that every chef gathers in his collection and depends on every day. These ones belong to David Burke, head chef at Wright Brothers Oyster and Porter House in London's Borough Market. David worked for me at Bibendum when it opened, before moving on to be a wonderful chef and director at Le Pont de la Tour, part of my gastrodrome on the River Thames beside Tower Bridge.

Pages 88–89 When we moved into the apartment above our office in Shad Thames in 1995, there was nothing here. In fact, we had to close off part of the atrium to make space for the kitchen. This now flows easily into the dining area, so that cooking and eating can be one seamless activity. The table is my design, made by Benchmark in ripple sycamore, and the chairs, made by a Czech company called Fischel in about 1880, have since been moved to the dining room at Barton Court.

Page 90 As well as having written about cooking in *The Sunday Times Magazine* for a year, my son Tom runs a successful café and provisions shop in London's Notting Hill Gate, a saloon bar and dining room called The Cow, and Lucky Seven, an American-inspired diner that has a marguerita lounge next door called Crazy Homies. In this picture by Debbie Treloar, he is instructing his daughter Iris in the art of cake icing.

Page 91 The kitchen in our apartment at Shad Thames is small but bright and airy, lit by daylight from the adjacent rooftop conservatory. Here, I'm serving Thai mussel soup, prepared with ginger, lemongrass, coriander, chilli, lime leaves and of course coconut milk. Before you serve, you discard any mussels that won't open.

Page 92 (Above) Who could resist a shop like this? This 1890s photograph shows a typical French provincial store in which you could buy everything under one roof. They were still popular throughout France when I went there in 1953 and became a major inspiration for Habitat, both in the products they sold and in the way the merchandise was presented.
(Below) Later, I discovered the quintessential E. de Hilleran shop in Les Halles in Paris. It still stocks the most comprehensive range of classic French kitchenware anywhere.

Page 93 The chicken brick, one of the products for which Habitat became famous for, was inspired by a visit to a restaurant in the middle of France where I had chicken that had been cooked in a pig's bladder; it retained the flavours wonderfully well. The concept of clay-pot cooking dates back to the ancient Etruscans and the Chinese. Cooking in this clay container is simplicity itself: season the bird to taste, replace the lid and put into a cold oven set at 250ºC (480ºF) for one and a half hours. The chicken browns itself miraculously inside the brick.

Page 94 When Habitat opened, it was not only the products, but the way in which they were displayed that made a huge impact. Rather than setting out one or two examples in a formal display, we had piles of products in our basement kitchen department and you could help yourself using supermarket-style wire baskets. This spectacular display was photographed in our French warehouse-cum-shop at Orgeval.

Page 95 This is not the sort of thing that every kitchen will have room for, but I like this extra-large stock pot – a prerequisite in every restaurant – for its simple no-nonsense design details and its metal finish. It reminds me of my early days in my first café, The Soup Kitchen, when we made soup in containers this size and kept them hot in *bain-maries*. We sold a pot of soup for one shilling and sixpence – not a bad deal.

Pages 96–97 In 2004 we designed an enormous range of homeware for the supermarket Sainsbury's, which we called 'bY'. It included everything from pots and pans to cutlery, kettles and toasters. It was based on the idea of informal eating and entertaining at home, so the shapes were stylish but simple and uncomplicated. This page of early ideas by my son Sebastian and Tris Keech, made in our design studio, shows the development of the pan shape and the trivet-cum-strainer lid.

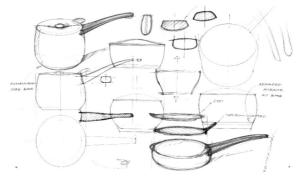

Page 98 This is my daughter Sophie with some of the range of over 100 pieces of cookware and tableware that she has created for Portmeirion Potteries. She works with a wide variety of companies on product development and design direction (including homeware and furniture) but at the same time she's also creating interior design concepts, writing cookery books, endorsing Aga cookers, and bringing up a young family. She is their inspiration, and mine, too.

Page 99 As you will have gathered, I like tableware that is plain and practical. I designed this collection of more than 50 pieces of kitchen and tableware for Royal Doulton. It is made from simple tactile materials such as oak, soda glass and wire, and the same wonderfully robust heat-retaining stoneware that was first developed by Doulton when it began in 1812. The shapes of the sauce jugs were inspired by birds.

Pages 100–101 This remarkable array of gleaming copper kettles and jelly moulds came from the kitchen at Raby Castle in County Durham. The castle was built in 1390 and the kitchen was in constant use for more than 600 years. All the woodwork in the room is painted this shade of blue, which was traditionally used to repel flies.

Page 102 Old photographs of kitchen staff, maids, stable boys and gardeners always fascinate me. They are an all-too-rare glimpse into a once thriving world of hardworking young people who started as apprentices and who devoted, in many cases, their whole lives to the support of grand English country houses and their families.

Page 103 Like a cathedral to cooking, this kitchen at Burghley House in Lincolnshire was built in the 1580s. Although no longer in use, the robust furniture and gleaming copper cookware are the sorts of things that have attracted my interest since I was a boy. I used to enjoy being taken to visit English country houses and was always drawn to the kitchens and the big, solid equipment that was used to produce food on a grand scale.

Page 104 I love pictures such as this, not only for the array of wonderful-looking fresh produce, but also because of the pride of the retailers and the graphic composition of the image. This photograph, taken in 1912, shows Moss Brothers' butcher's shop in Church Road, Willesden, London. Did the shop look like this every day? Maybe not, judging by the way a table has been covered with a sheet and placed on the pavement for extra display space.

Page 105 Looking like a painting by one of the Dutch masters, this piece of treacle-and-ale-cured bacon was photographed by Jean Cazals for our bi-annual magazine *Live It*. At the time, in 2004, we had just opened the Paternoster Chop House in the shadow of St Paul's Cathedral, a part of London where there were once a great many chop and ale houses. As a contrast to the trend for *nouvelle cuisine*, I wanted a place where you could order traditional robust English food and I wanted all of the produce sourced from butchers who dealt directly with British farmers.

Page 106 Baskets are some of my favourite things and I think these fish traps made by the Kuvirondo women in Kenya are absolutely beautiful. They are distinctive to their tribe and, like most handmade objects, have a grace and authenticity that is hard to replicate. They also make perfect sunshades. This photograph was taken by the Englishman Sir Harry Johnston in the early twentieth century.

Page 107 This photograph, taken in Brittany in 1900, encompasses lots of things I really like: freshly caught local seafood from French fishing villages; traditionally made baskets that have been designed for a specific purpose, like catching a particular type of fish or crustacean; simple wooden sailing boats; and the fisherman's *bleu de travail*, the blue workwear that you still see all over France.

Page 108 My kitchen garden is one of my greatest joys and early summer is one of the best times of year for vegetables. This little sketch I did shows some of my favourites: broad beans, artichoke, carrot, peas and radish. What could be more perfect?

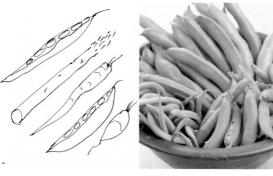

Page 109 A large bowl of peas and beans is a real treat, both visually and gastronomically. In their first youth, neither fava beans (broad beans) nor lima beans need shelling, but as they mature the pods become tough and should be discarded. They are best eaten when they have been plunged into rapidly boiling water and cooked until just tender, but not a moment longer.

Page 110 In the 1960s we adopted the idea of flat-pack furniture so that customers could assemble it themselves. It was quite a challenge because it had to be made with incredible precision. Packed flat in a cardboard box, furniture could be warehoused more neatly and despatched more economically but, most importantly, the customer could now have instant gratification, as the normal waiting time for new furniture was six to nine months. In these photographs, the carpenters are making 'Summa' kitchen units and tables.

Page 111 Our new factory in Thetford opened in 1963. It was designed by the Greater London Council's Architects' Department, but I had a very good relationship with the architect who was working on it and was able to tailor it to our needs. There was a showroom on the right for trade buyers and architects.

Page 112 During the 1960s and 1970s, we produced yearly Habitat Cook's and Gardener's Diaries written by a variety of writers and illustrated in different styles. For this edition from 1968, the 52 recipes were by my wife Caroline and the drawings were by the illustrator Agneta Neroth, whose work I still like.

eating

Page 114 In the 1960s Caroline and I moved the family to a beautiful four-storey Regency house in Regent's Park, London, that had been designed by Decimus Burton, an early nineteenth-century landscape architect. In the basement kitchen we kept a lot of the original features, including this old dresser with mismatched drawer handles. All family dinners, plus a lot of cooking and entertaining, happened down here. It was the beginning of the kitchen as family room – the heart of the home.

Page 116 This beautiful walnut cabinet, in which I display my collection of eighteenth-century English glass, is an old solicitors' cabinet. It has numbered pigeonholes where the briefs for each case were kept, and tiny drawers for files and documents.

Pages 118–119 This picture of Picasso by the French photographer Robert Doisneau was taken in the ceramics workshop in Villauris, where he was experimenting with ceramics in 1946, though his first painted cooking pots were made in 1906. Many of these vessels are the same shape, but the variety of decoration shows what fun he was having with what he described as the 'fourth dimension'. At the same time, we must remember that he was not only a decorator of plates and pots, but was constantly trying out different slips, oxides and glazes.

Page 120 I am not a big fan of floral arrangements, particularly the very contrived ikebana kind, but I love fresh flowers on my desk, around the house and in our restaurants. For me, the best presentation of flowers is one that looks natural, as if you have just brought them from the garden. When there are few flowers to be had outside, a big branch of blossom, crab apples or rose hips is just as good.

Page 122 Part sculpture, part giant utensil, this enormous bowl was made by Lars Zech. It measures 80cm by 45cm (32in by 18in). Zech works in a rudimentary workshop near the Black Forest in Germany using wood from 300-year-old trees that have been felled for disease or safety reasons. He first shapes the trunks into 800kg (126st) pieces with a chainsaw before fashioning them into bowls; it is an exhausting and delicate process. I love the idea of an artist working away in such a raw environment on such beautiful things.

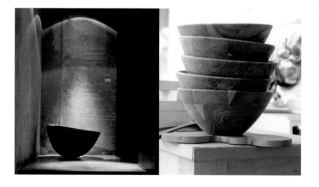

Page 115 This picture of a Victorian junk shop was taken by the British photographer John Thomson. By a strange coincidence, the chair in the picture is exactly the same design as the ones we had in our kitchen (opposite). I have always enjoyed rummaging around in these sorts of shops and often come across a great find. In fact, I was recently asked by the staff of a Japanese magazine to take them on a tour of flea markets and antiques shops in England and France.

Page 117 The simple display cabinet in our Shad Thames apartment was made to exactly the right proportions for the room by Benchmark and assembled in situ. I generally use it to store plates and bowls, things that are convenient for the dining table, so it is really the equivalent of an old-fashioned kitchen dresser.

Page 121 Like Picasso's pots, these ordinary mugs are transformed by their hand-painted designs. Mocha ware was produced in Staffordshire and Derbyshire from 1770 onwards using a variety of techniques. The dendritic (treelike) pattern (third row, left) was made by upending the vessel, dotting the wet slip with a few drops of tobacco or urine and using a blowpipe to create the effect. Although it was cheap, everyday pottery, real artisanship was required to achieve such fine decoration and it is now highly collectable.

Page 123 In India sheesham wood, or golden rosewood, is used extensively for furniture and handicrafts. It is easy to carve and has a lovely grain. These Conran Shop bowls were made in Moradabad in Uttar Pradesh in India using glued-together off-cuts to give a rich collage effect.

Page 124 This computer visual of a serving dish and salad bowl was part of a presentation we did for our clients Tchibo GmbH, the large Hamburg-based German retailer. Launched in February 2008, the 36cm (14 inches) diameter porcelain tableware was designed so that component pieces could be stacked together or used separately.

Page 125 I am amused by this array of Habitat products from 1965 and intrigued to see how many one would still buy today. Apart from the classics like the Le Creuset cookware, Sabatier knives and Anglepoise lamp, I can spot a garlic press, a cafetière and, of course, Elizabeth David's famous recipe books – all still very useful.

Page 126 David Mellor has been responsible for completely changing the image of British cutlery, initially with several very modern designs, and then with some beautifully classic ranges, most of which he has produced in his own Sheffield factory. My favourite is called, simply, 'English'. Designed in 1993, it was a development of the cutlery David had created for Downing Street, a commission that in the end did not go forward owing to a 'disagreement over aesthetics'. A story we have heard many times before, but rarely with such a fortuitous outcome.

Page 127 These table knives were made in Sheffield between 1760 and 1780. This was the era of a gradual but significant move of cutlery manufacturing from London to Sheffield, which had better power supplies, more available labour and a closer proximity to raw materials. The knives, an unwieldy 26cm (10½in) in length, have rounded scimitar-style iron blades and silver handles. They come from Sheffield's Bill Brown Collection, a remarkable assortment of some 1,200 utensils that date back 5,000 years.

Page 128 This is a display of our 'Summa' storage range and bentwood chairs in the Woolands Store in Knightsbridge, London, in 1963 (see page 293). It is classic Conran and predates what we were to do in the first Habitat a year later. At the time, few retailers would display your furniture in a coherent way and some – to our horror – never even bothered to take it out of the boxes or assemble it once it was delivered.

Page 129 The impact and the influence that Habitat had on the UK home when it opened on 11 May 1964, and the subsequent effect of the catalogues, has been written about again and again. One of the things that strikes me most now, when I look at this picture, is how lived-in the shop looks – as if you could just come in and sit down to lunch. The shop owed its success to a great deal of hard work by a very small team of people. In particular, I cannot overemphasise the tremendous work our display manager Morris Libby did for so many years.

Page 130 Beside the kitchen at Barton Court, the slightly more formal dining room is centred around a classic 1950s pedestal table by the Finnish designer Eero Saarinen. The lamp over the table, by Ingo Maurer (see page 241), gives as much light as we need, but Vicki might also add candles on occasion. The windows have deep insets and little window seats, so I have kept them free of heavy curtains. The colour comes from the rug, which I designed.

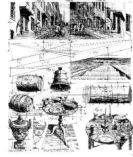

Page 131 This eighteenth-century drawing by the English architectural draughtsman Thomas Malton the Elder purports to show how perspective works, but I like it also for its idiosyncratic choice of household objects.

Page 132 Simple lacquered shelves extend the entire length of the chimneybreast in the dining room at Barton Court. Some of these serving tureens and jugs have been with me since our time in our house in Regent's Park in the 1970s, and contrary to the impression this picture gives, most of them are in constant use.

Page 133 'There is nothing inevitable about the appearance of manufactured objects. They didn't have to look this way.' I have always liked this sentence from the introduction to our first Boilerhouse Project exhibition in 1982 at London's Victoria and Albert Museum. (The Boilerhouse was the template of what was to become the Design Museum, now in Shad Thames). This photograph was taken at the Gustavsberg workshops just outside Stockholm in 1896.

Page 134 The creamware produced by the Leeds Pottery in the late 1700s is considered by some collectors to be the embodiment of eighteenth-century classicism. I am fascinated by this drawing from one of the factories' shape books, in which the draughtsman has illustrated different sizes of coffee pot within the one shape.

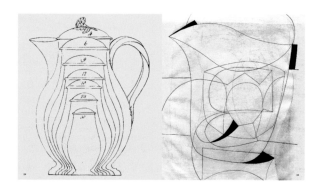

Page 135 The English artist Ben Nicholson often incorporated everyday objects into his drawings and paintings and, in this example, *1968 (green still life)*, his linear composition seems almost three-dimensional. 'All of his work signals an awareness of the artist's great dilemma – having to be coherent yet also free, sensible yet irrational. His work was not an investigation of it, yet he sometimes seems to be testing its limits' wrote Norbert Lynton in his book on Nicholson.

Page 136 Jugs and bowls like these were originally used for having a wash down in the bedroom, at a time when bathing in some households might have been a once-a-week event. I like them for their good shape and good decoration.

Page 137 I have always liked this 1920 Picasso painting, *Still Life with Jug and Apples*, for its colour and composition, and for the fact that he took the trouble to paint such a simple vessel. I read recently, however, that its fullness represents the shape of a woman's body and the handle is thought to be phallic, thus representing 'the union of male and female in the procreative act'. I couldn't possibly comment.

Page 138 When our restaurant Sartoria opened in Savile Row, London, in 1998, we used a selection of enormous white platters to serve antipasto at the bar. I am always drawn to the simple presentation – usually on white plates – of simply prepared food, something that I wish London's most talented young chefs today would adopt. Too often I find their food overdecorated and rather 'ditsy', with too many artistic flourishes. They should go back to Elizabeth David's exhortation: '*Fait simple*'.

Page 139 Buffets and picnics have never really appealed to me, but I love lunch outdoors, whether in one of our restaurants or at home. Beyond the dining room at Barton Court there is a courtyard garden with a big wooden-topped table and an assortment of chairs and benches that stay out all year round. For once, the table here was not set up for a photo shoot – Vicki took these pictures just before we all sat down for a very nice family lunch. Her sons Toby and Max are with my son Tom.

Page 140 Evoking many of the qualities I like about old French restaurants, Chartier in the rue du Faubourg in Paris was opened in 1896 to serve the well-known bouillon to blue-collar workers and the people of the neighbourhood. Sounds rather like my Soup Kitchens of 1954, though my waiters didn't wear *le Rodin* (a black waistcoat with many pockets) or long white aprons, and we had neither the fabulous glass ceiling nor the wooden racks with numbered drawers, where, in the early twentieth century, every customer kept his own napkin.

Page 141 Exhibited at London's Royal Academy Summer Show in 1969, this painting, *Diners*, by the English artist William Roberts, captures all the energy that goes into a popular restaurant. Roberts was an avid documenter of London life, painting ordinary people involved in their day-to-day activities at home, at work and at leisure, whether dining, swimming, dancing, going to the theatre – even playing snooker.

Page 142 My sister Priscilla and her husband Antonio Carluccio have created an inspiring chain of modern Italian caffés. This one in London's Spitalfields – their twenty-ninth – is on the ground floor of a modern residential building. The dining area seats 84 people in a bright, airy, colourful space adjacent to the 'Abundance of Food' retail area. The design is a joint effort between Priscilla, Simon McCarthy of Design LSM and Carluccio's development director, Alison Stanton.

Page 143 In the 1960s we did a big graphics programme for the wine company Harveys of Bristol, together with interiors for its shop and a restaurant in the cellars, which I was very proud of. When it acquired the Bath Oliver biscuit people Fortts of Bath in 1965, we were asked to design this restaurant in its big grocery shop. The white painted brickwork, natural materials, uncluttered lighting and classic bentwood-and-rattan chairs are all things I would still use today.

Page 144 I am not a very flamboyant person and I have never really been interested in showing off, but I love having a big grand staircase in my restaurants. This one is in Mezzo in London's Soho, but I created an even grander version in Quaglino's when we relaunched it in 1993. Incidentally, not entirely to my taste, Mezzo has now been totally redesigned and refitted, rather in the style of a Cuban bordello.

Page 145 This jolly 1930s drawing from the RIBA (Royal Institute of British Architects) archive was for the interior of Fischer's restaurant in New Bond Street, London. It was drawn by Raymond McGrath, the architect who – with Wells Coates and Serge Chermayeff – designed the interiors for the BBC's Broadcasting House in Portland Place in London. It successfully sums up many of the elements I have tried to include in my restaurants: comfortable chairs, diffused lighting, a grand staircase and plenty of happy customers.

Page 146 When I opened the Bluebird restaurant in King's Road, London in 1997, I commissioned Richard Smith to create a series of painted 'kites' to float in the huge lightwell above the restaurant. The artworks moved slightly in the circulating air and had the effect of adding a constantly changing element of colour to the otherwise monochromatic scheme. Sadly, the restaurant has been recently 'restyled', and the kites are now stored in the basement.

Page 147 I first met the painter Richard Smith in the 1960s, when he married Betsy, an old girlfriend of mine. Born in 1931, he was at the Royal College of Art in London with the artists Peter Blake and Joe Tilson, and at the forefront of the British Pop Art scene. Over the years, I have commissioned and bought many of his paintings. This picture was taken in his studio in Bath in 1970 by Jorge Lewinski, when Dick was working on a painting very like one that hung in our design office reception for a long time, and is now here at Barton Court. It is green.

Page 148 I have been working with Vicki and the restaurant consultant Peter Prescott on the Boundary Project, a refurbishment and extension of a listed Victorian industrial building in Shoreditch, East London. It is now a boutique hotel with 17 bedrooms, four of which are duplex suites with views of the city. This formal restaurant – The Boundary – in the lofty, daylight-filled basement serves high-quality, contemporary food in impressive surroundings. At the top of the building, there is a rooftop garden with a bar and grill.

Page 149 The ground floor of our building in Boundary Street is occupied by the Albion café, which serves robust, simple British meals, and also by a bakery and a food shop. It makes sense to me to give people plenty of choice – they can either sit down to a good meal or simply buy a freshly made sandwich.

Page 150 Now sadly destroyed, magnificent brick chimneys like these at Alfred Meakin's Royal Albert Works in Tunstall, Staffordshire, must have existed at all the Stoke-on-Trent potteries. When I was 16, one of my holiday jobs was to work for a month in Wrecclesham Potteries near Farnham, which meant cycling for 27km (17 miles) from home, then pedalling all day at the potter's wheel, and then pedalling home again. Later, David Queensberry told me he had worked there, too.

Page 151 I have a collection of coloured glass on the first-floor landing at Barton Court (see page 21). If I see a wine or liqueur bottle with lovely coloured glass, I keep it. Some of these might also be carafes.

Page 152 The inspiring thing about this manufacturer's catalogue page from the nineteenth century, is choice. When British manufacturers had the manpower and the flexibility – as well as the enterprise – to produce variety; retailers were able to choose from a wide number of designs and create their own exclusive ranges; and every shop didn't have the same stock. It's a fine example of how shops can and should be different.

Page 153 My son Tom and me in the wine cellars at Barton Court, a labyrinth of rooms that I use for storage and where Vicki has her printing press. They were used as the boys' changing rooms in the days when Barton Court was a school. This picture was shot for a recent magazine story, and might give the impression that I spend every evening down there carousing.

Pages 154–155 This remarkable sketch should be pinned to every furniture designer's wall. Drawn by the Danish furniture designer Kaare Klint around 1916, it is one of the most important documents in modern furniture development. Klint sought to rationalize and quantify the dimensional aspects of the human form and thereby calculate the physical requirements of the home. This was the first time anyone had studied the ergonomics of interior design and it pre-dated similar work by Le Corbusier and the American product designer Henry Dreyfuss by some 30 years.

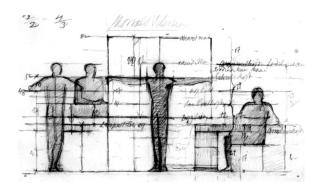

Page 156 The 'C114' was one of a series of office chairs that we made at our Thetford factory in 1966. It was designed by the Finnish designers Olli Mannermaa, Voitto Haapalainen and Kay Ko/rbing, we bought the polystyrene seat shells in Finland and made the rest ourselves. There were several versions, including one with arms, which we used extensively in office projects, including our own.

Page 157 The Royal Festival Hall was at the heart of the 1951 Festival of Britain on the South Bank of the Thames in London, and the entire building has recently undergone a gentle refurbishment. Our part of the project was to redesign and refit the restaurant, now called Skylon. The huge space, with its 6m- (20ft-) high ceilings and river views was unified by the use of heritage colours, which were part of the original scheme, and chandeliers with aluminium fins finished in bronze. As a homage to the period, we used Eero Saarinen's 'Executive' chairs.

Page 158 It was a brilliant eighteenth-century idea to elevate the simple dining chair to a status symbol. If you were furnishing your home, you could choose from dozens of variations of chairbacks in the Chinese, rococo and classical styles. Chairs were often made by individual local craftsmen working from designs in lavish furniture catalogues that were produced by the great furniture designers of the day: George Hepplewhite, Thomas Sheraton, Thomas Chippendale, Thomas Hope and George Smith.

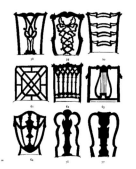

Page 159 Using some of the same design features and construction techniques as the famous Sussex range that William Morris designed for Morris, Marshall, Faulkner & Co. in the early 1900's, this country-made chair is one of several I've had and admired for many years.

Page 160 I greatly admire the Shakers because they believed in a life of simplicity and order, and their furniture is famous for its clean lines and lack of unnecessary embellishment. In their homes they aimed to create 'space, beauty, symmetry and the light and splendour of a summer's day'. To make cleaning easier and more thorough, they fixed a peg rail around their rooms at head height on which to hang chairs. They excelled at fine craftsmanship and artistic expression was encouraged.

Page 161 Behind me on the wall of my 1956 showroom are some ladder-back chairs that I was importing from Chiavari in the Italian Gulf of Genova. I still have one in my office today. Incredibly light and elegant, with rush seats woven by the wives of fishermen, the design inspired the Italian designer Gio Ponti to create his 'Superleggera' chair, which was supposed to be the weight of a paperclip.

Page 162 Using green oak sourced on Dartmoor, this enormous chair was made by the local woodworker and sculptor Henry Bruce. His idea was that the chair would draw attention to the view in the way that an ordinary bench does, while at the same time creating a frame for it. This, he hoped, would give people pause to stop and appreciate the beautiful natural surroundings. Mindful of the impact the piece would have on the environment, he built it using traditional mortise-and-tenon technology and hewed it by hand.

Page 163 The Japanese home and lifestyle magazine *Casa Brutus* has commissioned me over the years to explore shops, factories and flea markets in various parts of the world and select for their readers items that meet my style and quality criteria. This enormous Chippendale-style chair was discovered in an antiques shop in Isle-sur-la-Sorgue in France. It made me smile.

Page 164 From the many trade catalogues and household documents in the archive of the Geffrye Museum in East London, this is a page of wooden baluster designs from the Stratford company Young & Marten Ltd. It fascinates me because of the abundance of choice that was available to house builders in the late 1850s, and the fact that all the balusters were in stock 'ready to despatch on receipt of order'.

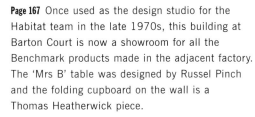

Page 165 Enjoying a renaissance today, this type of turned table leg was popular in Britain during the Victorian period, but I found these in a book on indigenous Australian furniture called *Memories* by Graham Cornall. Although reflecting European influences, to experts their rhythm and proportion distinguish them as Western Australian Jarrah turnings from 1860–1890.

Page 166 I was 25 when this picture was taken in 1956 and I had set up a showroom selling my furniture and printed textiles in a converted stable in Cadogan Place in London. I would zip back and forth between there, my furniture factory in Donne Place and the Soup Kitchen (which I ran at night) on my pale green Vespa. It was perfect for the job and I even delivered some of the furniture on the back of it.

Page 167 Once used as the design studio for the Habitat team in the late 1970s, this building at Barton Court is now a showroom for all the Benchmark products made in the adjacent factory. The 'Mrs B' table was designed by Russel Pinch and the folding cupboard on the wall is a Thomas Heatherwick piece.

Page 168 We have a team of nearly 50 working in the Benchmark factory, nearly three-quarters of whom came direct from school via our apprenticeship scheme, and many of whom stay for life. Our oldest member is Steven Huzzey, who joined when he was 15 and is now a co-director. We produce commercial furniture in the workshop, including fit-outs for restaurants, hotels and offices, as well as domestic furniture for private clients.

Page 169 Modern tubular-steel furniture occupies a unique place in the history of furniture design and manufacture, evoking a certain culture of the 1920s and 1930s that accompanied the brave new world of modern art, architecture and the machine age. In this picture from the 1933–1934 catalogue of the Rotterdam manufacturer Gispen, factory workers demonstrate the strength of the tubular-steel table legs.

Page 170 I remember the time that Tony Snowdon came down to stay at Barton Court in 1982 and took this and many other photographs. I was rather irritated that he got up at five in the morning and changed all the furniture around to suit his compositions.

sleeping

Page 172 In a copy of a book on the architecture of the great Italian Andrea Palladio, the eighteenth-century English architect George Dance the Younger (or someone in his office) has pasted some sketches for projects he was working on, giving us a tantalizing glimpse into the work of a great man. This page contains ceiling designs, one of which has been filled in with watercolours.

Page 173 Two of the things that appealed to me about Barton Court when I first saw it were the proportions of the rooms and the abundance of original features that had survived its life as a school. This is one of two large bedrooms on the first floor. The Indian miniature paintings are part of a collection I bought during a trip there 40 years ago.

Page 174 Painted on cloth, this splendid *picchavai* from Rajasthan was made in the late nineteenth century to hang behind a famous figure of the god Krishna in a temple in Mewar, north of Udaipur. It depicts in beautiful detail a plan of the *haveli* of Shrinathji (Krishna) during the Annakut festival, and was shown recently at the Francesca Galloway Gallery in London. Rajasthan is famous for its craftsmen and women and has long been a destination for buyers in search of its wonderful textiles, paintings and other handicrafts.

Page 175 In the town of Jaisalmer in Rajasthan, this Durbar Hall is part of the Nathamal *haveli*, which was built in 1885 by the local ruler Maharwal Beri Sal Singh as a gift for his prime minister. With an arcaded corridor leading to windows on to the street and a delicately carved balcony, the room is richly decorated with hand-painted floral patterns, Mughal miniatures and framed nineteenth-century prints.

Page 176 A brilliant product development director, Polly Dickens has worked with me on merchandise for The Conran Shop on and off since 1981. One of her recent tasks was to investigate contemporary design in India and find young people who are working with traditional crafts. For this project, called Kantha, the young textile designer Neeru Kumar (top) is working with women in rural Bengal to produce embroidered patchwork quilts.

Page 177 Although many women in India are employed in the pottery industry, they are rarely allowed to work the clay on the wheel because, according to the Indian designer Puente Barr, 'it creates a phallic form that is considered objectionable'. Working in Pondicherry on a collection for The Conran Shop recently, she devised box-shaped vessels and bowls that could be made by pressing clay into a mould. Thus women from poorer communities can 'have a feeling of dignity by participating more in the country which has moved on and left them behind'.

Page 178 In our bedroom at Barton Court, this twist on the ubiquitous chest of drawers is a Benchmark piece made in mocha-stained oak. The sycamore doors slide open and although it can be two-sided, it seemed to me to make an ideal shirt cupboard placed here against the wall. On top is a cluster of early English pottery jugs.

Page 179 Above our bed is a framed Persian textile that, when we repainted the house a few years ago, inspired me to use yellow on the walls. The colour has worked well and gives the room a cheerful glow in the mornings. The 1930s desk and chair are in the style of the French furniture and interior designer Pierre Chareau, and I designed the folding mirror; the bed, too, is one of my designs for The Conran Shop.

Page 180 This is my reinvention of the old Louis Vuitton travelling trunk or portmanteau that rich folk took with them when they 'did' Europe or went on one of those elegant 1920s cruises. The shelves are made of zinc and I use it as a sort of dressing table when I am in London. It is an absolutely fiendish place to lose things in, however.

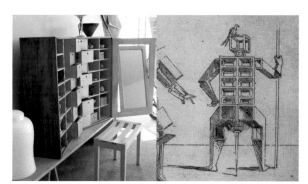

Page 181 From a portfolio by the seventeenth-century Florentine painter and engraver Giovanni Battista Braccelli, this engraving is one of his fascinating drawings of the human form constructed from a variety of animate and inanimate components. Only discovered in modern times, it reminds me of the work of Dada and the Surrealists and, more recently, of the Dutch designer Tejo Remy, whose 'Chest of Drawers' is made from a collection of old 'found' drawers haphazardly piled together.

Page 182 I like curvy bentwood *chaise-longues* as a contrast to rather more severe pieces and you will often find one in my rooms. I have always been excited and thrilled by the work of the nineteenth-century Viennese furniture maker Michael Thonet, partly because he solved so many construction problems with his bentwood technology. His chairs are not only comfortable, but also flexible, and so strong that if they are dropped in transit they will not break or come apart.

Page 183 A similar spectacular adjustable bentwood *chaise* now sits in one of the bedrooms at our London apartment in Shad Thames. Set against a backdrop of sheer white curtains, it provides a peaceful place in which to relax and read. For simplicity, the curtain headings have been set into the ceiling. The wall of windows behind it looks out on to a side canal and converted dockland warehouses.

Page 184 Michael Thonet invented the technique of bending solid wood with steam in the 1850s. He went on to create a large range of light, strong, flexible and timeless furniture, which he successfully mass-produced. I have admired and collected Thonet furniture since the 1950s. He was awarded a prize at the London Exhibition of 1862, where the judges declared his technique 'an excellent application of a happy thought'.

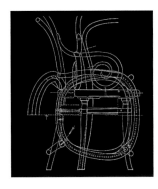

Page 185 This 1873 sales catalogue for Thonet's Viennese company, Gebrüder Thonet, remains a testament to the ingenuity and variety of the bentwood technique. With outlets in Paris, London and New York, the company even offered folding stools and walking sticks.

Page 186 What I was trying to do in this picture for *Elle Decoration* was show how to take old bits of junk-shop furniture – these were Utility designs from the 1940s – and, by removing the varnish and replacing the handles, transform them into very nice contemporary pieces of bedroom furniture for very little money. The chair is by Alberto Lievore from The Conran Shop and the shirts were 'designer's own'.

Page 187 Catering for travellers who want somewhere inexpensive to stay for a few hours or overnight, this premium short-stay room is one of 36 such facilities operated at Gatwick Airport by Yotel. Each yacht-style cabin has a power shower, internationally compatible plugs, internet access and an electrically adjustable sofa bed. The British designer Paul Priestman did the concept work for Yotel, and we did the design development and implementation at Conran & Partners.

Page 188 While the children were growing up, there was a constant flow of artists and creative people staying in the house: Howard Hodgkin, Francis Bacon, Richard Smith, Dicky Chopping, Dennis Wirth-Miller, David Hockney and, of course, Eduardo Paolozzi, so I expect it was inevitable that one of our children would be a painter. This is some of my son Ned's work from his recent show at the Shreik gallery. Clockwise from top left: *The Unplayable Game, The Viking Demographic, When I Was a Lad* and *They'll be Queuing.*

Page 189 While I was studying at the Central School of Arts and Crafts in London, Anton Einzig, who taught us screen-printing, had a workshop in Shepherd Market and I had a night job with him. We did work for the Czech textile designer Zika Ascher, printing scarves with designs by contemporary artists, and one day a job came in to print 10 or 12 big panels of natural-coloured linen with cutwork patterns in white pigment by Matisse. There was a terrible temptation to misprint one and take it home. This 1946 picture is of the same design, used as panels in Matisse's Paris studio.

Page 190 David Hockney's *Water Pouring into Swimming Pool, Santa Monica 1964*, a print of which hangs in the bathroom at Barton Court, was one of his investigations into the visual aspects of water. His agent Kasmin and I have been great friends for many years. He was my partner when I opened the Neal Street Restaurant in 1971 and we got David to do a drawing of the table setting, which we used for the menu. The original hung in the front bar until the restaurant closed in 2007.

bathing

Pages 192–193 I have always loved the idea of a very big bathroom and a very big bath. Luckily, I found this tub with its marble slab underneath it when I renovated Barton Court. On the wall, when this picture was taken, I had a little collection of works by friends, including Howard Hodgkin, David Hockney and Richard Smith. On the floor there were cork tiles, which back then were *de rigueur* for every bathroom, and indeed, many kitchens.

Pages 194–195 Over the years, this room at Barton Court, next to our bedroom, has gone through several transformations, but I have always kept the open fire, the old-fashioned style bathtub and the capacious storage, which is currently concealed behind floor-to-ceiling mirrored doors.

Page 196 This bathroom is used mainly by the children, who stay in the rooms on the top floor of the house where there are wonderful views from the windows. Cupboards are concealed behind wall-to-wall mirrors above the basins and the chair is vintage Lloyd Loom.

Page 197 The twin bowls in our bathroom were made from the same rich brown travertine as the rest of the room. Given the shape of the bowls, I guess it was almost inevitable that I made the bevelled mirrors round, too. The new floor is of Austrian-engineered oak.

Pages 198–199 I was delighted when I found this wonderful brown travertine marble for our bathroom because normally travertine is light beige. The Italian company that supplies it came over specially to install it on site, which took about a week. I rather like the incision beside the shower, and it's practical as well, because I had to leave a gap behind the wall to take all the water and waste pipes.

Page 200 Still in the bathroom, I have installed this very thin shelf to hold a collection of beautiful brushes that I found in a shop in SoHo in New York. Some, with long goat-hair bristles and turned-wood handles, were barber's brushes or writing desk brushes, while others may have been used for cleaning, priming and painting.

Page 201 The ultimate in door-to-door selling, what could be more thrilling than the sight of a vendor like this coming down your street? Now almost entirely disappeared from the UK, independent retailers like this still operate in parts of India, Africa and the Far East, mainly selling fruit and vegetables, though on Lake Nageen in Kashmir they come round in boats filled with housewares, groceries, fruit and fresh flowers.

Page 202 In my London office one wall is covered entirely in framed illustrations from a brush manufacturer. Not only do I love the simple functional shapes of the products, but the composition of the groups reminds me of some of the things we did in the very first Habitat catalogues in the 1970s.

Page 203 There is a wonderful antiquarian bookseller in London called David Batterham who sometimes gets portfolios of illustrations, cartoons or trade catalogues. I have used some in my restaurants Le Pont de la Tour and Bibendum. He found this portfolio of products from a French brush manufacturer. He thought 'Terence would like those' – and indeed Terence did.

Page 204 The Japanese art of bathing, and its ritual of inducing a sense of serenity, has inspired designers and ecologists for years, not least the British architect John Pawson and French designer Philippe Starck. In this early twentieth-century photograph, girls soak in a deep wooden barrel, though quite how they got in and out is a mystery.

Page 205 There can be few natural shapes as sensual as the egg and, like the shell of an egg, the shells of bathroom ceramics must be smooth, supportive and protective of the body in its vulnerable naked state. Based on this principle, the 'Aveo' range of bathroom fittings was designed by Conran & Partners for Villeroy & Boch in 2003 and won several prestigious awards.

Page 206 This wonderful bathroom, with its solid carved marble tub, was designed in 1905 by Josef Hoffmann (see page 243) for the Palais Stoclet in Brussels. It is a masterful blend of luxury and functional simplicity. I love the combination of dark and light marble and the generous wooden-framed daybed where one might have a post-bathtime nap or, indeed, a little light massage.

Page 207 My London bathroom has my favourite old-style bathtub, for which I designed a modern timber plinth. Beside it is a table with all the usual unguents decanted into beautiful old bottles and carafes. The bespoke marble basin was made in Italy and the mirror has etched discs through which light passes from the cupboards behind.

Page 208 Inspired, he says, by the sofa featured in the film *Breakfast at Tiffany's*, together with a passion for recycling spent household objects, the British designer Max McMurdo creates witty *chaises* from damaged roll-top bathtubs that he and his team find on building sites. 'Whenever we can, we contact the developers to see if they will let us remove them carefully before they get broken up and chucked out. It's only those beyond restoration that we convert.' By cutting away the side, the elegant shape of the fitting is accentuated.

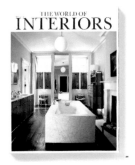

Page 209 This is the New York brownstone home of the American actress Julianne Moore and her husband Bart Freundlich as featured on the cover of *The World of Interiors* in 2006. To my surprise and amusement, I see in their bathroom a cabinet that looks very similar to those I was making in about 1960, though they tell me that in fact it is by the French designer Pierre Guariche. At any rate, I have always read and loved this magazine, and have found it full of inspiration, ever since the day my ex-pupil Min Hogg launched it in 1981.

Page 210 Vicki took this photograph from a friend's helicopter and I like it because it shows the way my plan for the walled garden has turned out. On the left there is the cutting garden and herbs, in the centre are the vegetables and four London plane trees, and on the right are the caged soft fruits.

growing

Page 212 When food was rationed in World War II, people were encouraged to cultivate every spare bit of land. This photograph from 1942 shows the allotments tended by the firemen of the Redcross Street Fire Station amid the bomb-damaged ruins of the City of London. St Paul's Cathedral can be seen in the background. These days it seems that allotment gardening is becoming popular again and a new generation is discovering the joy to be had from growing your own vegetables.

Page 213 I like this almost schematic representation of Llanerch Hall in Denbighshire; it is part landscape painting, part planning diagram, part status symbol. There is a whole school of this type of art from the seventeenth century and this picture shows the Italianate house and grounds as they were between 1662 and 1672. Llanerch Hall was recently awarded a £28,000 grant by the Welsh Assembly to carry out essential roof repairs, so I expect the garden needs some TLC too.

Pages 214–215 Looking towards the house, this series tells the whole story. My gardener Jon Chidsey took the snow picture in 2007 and my design assistant Stuart Westwell carried on the idea. Jon came to us when he was 16 and has run the garden for nearly 30 years. He was responsible for adding the herb garden and I get enormous pleasure from talking to him and planning new ideas. When it comes to the heavier things like mowing and fence mending, he has the help of Dean Husk. Looking at these views, I think I like spring best, when things are coming to life.

Pages 216–217 How nice to see children surrounded by garden produce. This charming image flies in the face of the current preoccupation with snacks, ready meals and junk food, and brings to mind the inspirational work that Jamie Oliver has been doing in teaching school children to appreciate fresh fruit and vegetables. Photographed in 1936, these children were from the Leytonstone branch of the Homeless Children's Aid and Adoption Society, enjoying their Harvest Festival gifts.

Page 218 Growing up, we often spent family holidays by the sea, on the Isle of Wight or at Feltham near Littlehampton, where this picture of me playing 'air' cricket may have been taken. In fact, I was probably responsible for starting World War II, because I once hit the German ambassador von Ribbentrop's son over the head with my spade when he walked over a sandcastle I had just built.

Page 219 I expect my mother, or maybe our nanny, took this picture of me and my sister Priscilla outside our house when we were living just off the Finchley Road in North London around 1935. It was a smallish garden, but big enough for bonfire parties. My furry friend was a dog called Nelson, or 'Nelly Bags'. For a long time he was at Barton Court, but I recently sent him to the Imperial War Museum for an exhibition about British children during the war.

Page 220 There is a long tradition of artists who painted exquisite still-lifes of fruit and vegetables, such as the Flemish painter Joachim Beuckelaer in the sixteenth century and the Spanish Francisco Zurbarán in the seventeenth. Some of my favourite works are by Sánchez Cotán, whose colours and forms possess an intense clarity. I have picked this painting by the Flemish artist Lucas Van Valckenborch from the sixteenth century, because it combines traders and shoppers in the market square with an abundance of delicious-looking produce.

Page 221 My first impressions of French rural markets, which I encountered in 1953, have always stayed with me. These wonderful displays of fresh produce make you long to cook and eat the delicious-looking fruit and vegetables, but I also find them very exciting aesthetically. The neatness and simplicity of presentation in these kinds of markets all over the world has always been a great inspiration to me.

Page 222 A tiny still-life of different kinds of bean, this stamp is one of a series called 'Crops of the Americas' issued in America in 2006. Other stamps depicted corn, chilli peppers and squash. The American artist Steve Buchanan used as reference his wife Rita's research into indigenous agricultural methods in the south-western states.

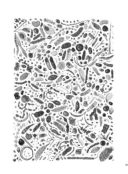

Page 223 This spectacular watercolour painting took the natural history illustrator Rachel Pedder-Smith 94 painting days to complete and shows the seeds from 530 specimens of the *Leguminosae*, or pea and bean, family from the Herbarium Collection at the Royal Botanic Gardens in Kew, where the painting now hangs.

Page 224 There is a long tradition in this country of gardeners competing to grow the largest or the most perfect specimens of fruit and vegetables and presenting them to be judged at local agricultural shows and fairs. During the war, this was propelled into a national obsession with the 'Dig for Victory' campaign, as everyone (us included) was encouraged to dig up their lawns to grow food. This is John Hall, an 89-year-old London gardener with his prize-winning vegetables, on 9 October 1942.

Page 226 Suttons Seeds was founded in 1806 to supply corn and in 1837 began selling flower and vegetable seeds from its shop in the market place in Reading. Now an internationally renowned supplier, it has enjoyed royal patronage since Queen Victoria used its seeds and plants in 1858. These collectable cards were issued by the company to customers in the nineteenth century and we reproduced them in the 1970s to create a wrapping-paper design that we sold in Habitat.

Pages 228–229 Seen in 1992 against a snowy land-scape, Henry Moore's *Reclining Figure* and *Sheep Piece* seem even more dramatic in their setting at Perry Green, his home in Hertfordshire. The thing I love about his sculpture is that it is so organically romantic. It does not seem to be within the English character, but he was living up to Picasso, Braque, and Brassaï. I met him in 1949 when we printed one of his textile designs for scarves.

Page 230 Beside the house at Barton Court there is an area where all the sewers run. The ground is very poor and gravelly and nothing would grow there, so 20 years ago I planted box and yew, which likes poor soil, and began to create this topiary. Beyond is a small caravan that was salvaged from a display we did once at The Conran Shop. Now it is the favourite playhouse of my grandchildren, who call it Jeremy Clarkson.

Page 232 On my first trip to France I was introduced to the *quincaillerie*, the French word for an ironmongery shop. I discovered wonderful straight-forward agricultural tools and garden equipment, which were then not available in the UK. They seemed to combine great sculptural qualities with durability and fitness for purpose.

Page 225 I love having fresh vegetables at my fingertips and have often said how much I enjoy wandering into the garden – or sending Vicki – before supper to pick whatever happens to be just ready to eat. In fact, in 1999 I designed a chef's roof garden at the Chelsea Flower Show, and it won a gold medal. These, by the way, are delicious little French breakfast radishes.

Page 227 Taken in a Tokyo market by the great French photographer Gilles de Chabaneix, this photograph reminds me of the boxes of fresh fruit, vegetables and herbs that we send from our garden to our London restaurants once or twice a week, from May to October.

Page 231 From the Lindley Library at the Royal Horticultural Society in London, this topiary illustration comes from a book of original engravings of German and French gardens dated 1717–1730. It is by Matthias Diesel, an eighteenth-century garden architect who worked in Passau, Salzburg, Regensburg and throughout Bavaria. My own topiary is rather more robust than this.

Page 233 Topiary like this requires not only a sense of humour, but infinite patience and long-term vision. Photographed in 1962 by Nancy Sirkis, this remarkable example was considered one of the great gardens of Newport, Rhode Island. The private garden was tended by the 80 year-old Miss Brayton, assisted by her full-time gardener George Mendonca, but it was planted a century earlier by Miss Brayton's grandfather.

Page 234 I love the dual purpose of this well-made wheelbarrow, which doubles as a garden seat. 'Juliett' is the brainchild of the Birmingham designer Chris Eckersley who recalls, 'I had the idea when I picked up a postcard at the Minack Open Air Theatre in Cornwall. It showed the theatre's creator, Rowena Cade, as an old lady sitting in an upturned builder's barrow. I was immediately inspired to produce a more comfortable modern version.'

Page 235 The great Victorian Isambard Kingdom Brunel was a designer, an engineer and a perfectionist. As well as creating magnificent bridges, tunnels, ships and railways, he also designed railway engines – and this wheelbarrow for Wearmouth Dock in Sunderland, for which he was the engineer. On 5 December 1831 he wrote of the advances in steam power: 'The time is not far off when we shall be able to take our coffee and write while going noiselessly and smoothly at 45mph.'

Page 236 Another of those objects that I have had for ages (see page 35), this painted tin hand – English, I guess – was once the tradesman's sign that hung outside a glove maker's shop. Behind it rest a series of my brother-in-law Antonio's meticulously carved hazel-wood walking sticks.

Page 237 The rapidly emerging buds of our indoor hippeastrum bulbs are a joy to behold. Even before they burst into flower on the table in the kitchen, they look striking. My favourites are the white ones with a hint of green, such as 'Green Goddess', or the brilliant 'Red Lion', but I have also recently discovered the spectacular 'Papilio', or butterfly amaryllis.

Page 238 My family used to have a collection of these beautiful seventeenth-century still-life flower paintings, but they sold them to pay for my and my sister's school fees. This one, dated 1661, with its attendant moths and butterflies, is by the Flemish artist Jan van Kessel the Elder.

Page 239 Another still-life, but this is a photograph, taken by the talented Howard Sooley, of the beautiful parrot tulip 'Rococo'. Flowers, in bud or fully open, are a source of constant study and inspiration, and I like nothing more than taking a walk around my garden, noticing what is coming up or what is just out in bloom. At the end of a busy or frustrating day, it is the best way to clear one's head.

Page 240 The contorted form of this extraordinary-looking Japanese plant has a certain mysterious elegance. The flowers of *Arisaema kiushianum* are only 8cm (3in) high and last for about three weeks in May. They were originally found on the wooded hillsides of Japan, but this one and a variety of others, equally strange, come from Jacques Armand's nursery in Middlesex.

Page 241 I love the work of the German lighting designer Ingo Maurer and I have several of his lamps in Barton Court. This design, 'Gaku', comes from his 'Mamo Nouchies'® series, which was created as a homage to the Japanese-American designer Isamu Noguchi, famous for his mulberry paper and bamboo light sculptures. The delicate forms are made by folding and pulling paper, a process invented by Dagmar Mombach with the technical assistance of Hagen Sczech and the team at Ingo Maurer.

Page 242 Fritillaria are some of my favourite flowers, particularly 'Meleagris', which comes up all over our garden in April. The little chequerboard flowers remind me of Josef Hoffmann's designs for the Wiener Werkstätte. They would certainly make a beautiful textile pattern. This 1915 watercolour is by the great Scottish architect and designer Charles Rennie Mackintosh, who was also clearly inspired by them.

Page 243 I have always admired the work of the Austrian architect and designer Josef Hoffmann. This two-tier fruit stand was one of his metalware designs produced in 1904 for the pioneering Wiener Werkstätte, the craft workshops he co-founded in 1903, and for which he designed furniture and decorative objects for nearly 30 years. He once said, 'The purpose of all architects and designers should be to break away from the historicist stranglehold of the museums and to create a new style.'

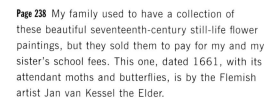

Page 244 Whatever the time of year, there always seems to be something interesting to see or do in our greenhouses, and often something to eat. Totally restored from the rotting and abandoned state that I found them in, they were at one time filled with exotic orchids, but now we grow early salads, potatoes, carrots, French breakfast radishes and French beans, as well as germinating all the seedlings for the vegetable garden.

Page 245 The delicate watercolours of Eric Ravilious are full of his observations of the seemingly ordinary aspects of England between the wars. He was a talented painter, illustrator and designer, and later turned his hand to designing furniture, china and glassware. This picture, *Carnation House*, from 1938, appeals to me for its subject matter and for its strong sense of composition: notice how he has slightly bowed the upright frames, giving the painting an almost photographic distortion.

Page 246 On a table in the dining room, these little greenhouses remind me of the seedling house I am building on top of the Boundary Street project (see pages 148–149). It is for the chef, so that he can grow seedlings of any new herbs or vegetable varieties he might come across when he is abroad. We will then find growers who can carry on producing these new crops for us. I have also just designed a cloche for the cheese trolley in the restaurant there, inspired by them.

Page 247 Many of the great country houses of the eighteenth and nineteenth centuries had greenhouses and conservatories for growing exotic fruits and plant specimens. This magnificent conservatory, begun in 1832, is at Harlaxton Manor near Grantham, Lincolnshire. Sir Gregory Gregory, who commissioned the building, considered home improvement his primary diversion, 'as hunting or shooting or feasting may be the objects of other people'.

Page 248 This is R. Buckminster Fuller, the famous American designer, architect and inventor, and some of his students at Black Mountain College, North Carolina, in the United States. Here, they are testing the strength of one of his first necklace geodesic domes in 1949. Fuller's inspired theory was based on the calculation that as the dome's diameter increased, the force on individual struts decreased, and the diffusion of force became more and more effective, thus enabling the construction of large-scale domes and creating a new way to span space.

Page 249 At the Eden Project in Cornwall, Buckminster Fuller's technology has been used to create two giant greenhouses called Biomes. Made from tubular-steel hexagons covered with transparent foil, the biggest Biome is 55m (180ft) high, 100m (330ft) wide and 200m (660ft) long. The brainchild of businessman Tim Smit and architect Jonathan Bell, the site was designed and developed by the architect Nicholas Grimshaw. Its purpose is to promote understanding of the relationship between plants and humans and it contains specimens of more than 5,000 species.

Page 250 Besides the sphere, the egg must be one of the most aesthetically satisfying and beautiful shapes, quite apart from the variety of delicate colours and patterns one finds in birds' eggs. The American food writer and publisher Martha Stewart based a whole collection of house paints on the hues of her hens' eggs. This lovely speckled one is a gull's egg.

passions

Page 252 One of the threads running through my career is the practice of breathing new life into beautiful old 'ladies', taking old buildings and transforming them for new uses, as shops, restaurants, hotels or, indeed, homes. In fact, apart from my factories and warehouses, and projects for Design Group clients, I don't think I have ever worked with new-build schemes. This is The Conran Shop in Paris, occupying part of the building that the engineer Gustave Eiffel built with architect Louis-Charles Boileau for the department store Au Bon Marché in 1887.

Page 253 From the days when we opened the first Habitat shop on Fulham Road, London, I had always admired the Michelin Building opposite and I finally bought it in 1985. Together with Paul Hamlyn, we set about restoring the tiling and reinstated some of the stained-glass windows and illuminated glass turrets. It became the headquarters of Hamlyn Publishing, and The Conran Shop moved there in 1987.

Page 254 This is a page of my pencil sketches for a range of Bibendum-style ceramics and glassware. I did a few things when we opened the restaurant, but I've always thought that a larger collection of tableware based on his exuberant characteristics would be a natural.

Page 255 Long before I bought the Michelin Building, I had been fascinated by the company's logo, Monsieur Bibendum. Some say it represents me – fat and jolly and always smoking a cigar but I am not so sure.

Page 256 This is part of the forecourt floor mosaic in the Bibendum Restaurant, which is perhaps the least compromised restaurant as regards my personal taste, and the one I am most proud of. Apart from the Hoffmann chairs in the waiting area, I designed almost all the furniture and most of the fittings myself, including the glassware and china. The Mr Bibendum ashtrays, which were stolen in their hundreds, have now become butter dishes since the no-smoking legislation.

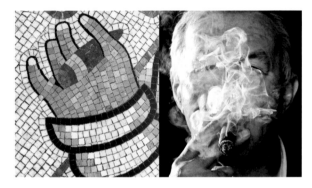

Page 257 I remember I smoked my first cigar on the opening night of Habitat on 11 May 1964. It was given to me by my friend and colleague Oliver Gregory, who said that in America it was traditional for every father to smoke a cigar on the birth of a child. Since then, I have not looked back. I now smoke a Havana cigar called Hoyo de Monterrey, which I have found to be mild enough to be enjoyed at any time from after breakfast to just before bed, accompanied in the evening by a glass of Vieille Prune.

Page 258 Living in the country, as we did during the war, presented rich opportunities for a budding creative. Not only did I experiment with welding and building my own pottery kiln, but there were also plenty of fascinating *objets trouvés* to salvage. Priscilla, who was studying photography, took this picture of me with a sculptural piece of farm machinery.

Page 259 Throughout my home, I have things that are a particular inspiration to me and this is one of them. It is a metal sculpture, signed 'par Aolossi – Arles 2004', and I like it because it hovers halfway between art and artefact.

Page 260 I never really understood the Burj Al Arab Hotel on Jumeirah Beach in Dubai, with its spectacularly kitsch interior, until I saw this photograph of Subodh Kerkar's sculpture of upturned boats, called *The Sea Remembers*. It is a good example of how inspiration can come from anywhere and how our eyes can be opened by seeing things in a new way or from a different point of view.

Page 261 Soaring like a great sail above Portsmouth harbour, the Spinnaker Tower, designed by Hedley Greentree, has rightly become a new iconic landmark for the town and has helped to regenerate the old quays. The 170m- (558ft-) high viewing tower houses three glass-enclosed viewing platforms and has been described by some as 'one of the most spectacular design projects of the decade'. The design was chosen by the readers of *The Portsmouth News* from three different proposals and has been a great success in providing 'an uplifting experience'.

Page 262 Traditional fishing boats have, by nature, a purely functional purpose and I find their practical design detailing truly inspirational. When it came to the top-floor terrace of our Shad Thames apartment, I wanted to create some shade and filter the light coming into the rooms, as well as adding a bit of sexiness to what is quite an austere building. I came up with the idea of a sail, which softens the large terrace area, and links it to the Thames near by.

Page 263 When I was little, many of our holidays were spent at the seaside, and I have always had a strong affinity with the sea. I love the work of the British artist Christopher Wood, a friend of Winifred and Ben Nicholson (see page 135), whose naïve paintings encapsulate everything I like about fishing boats and the unspoilt harbours of Cornwall and Brittany. This drawing, *Fishing Boat, Dieppe*, was done in 1929, the year before his death at the young age of 29. Kettle's Yard (see page 63), has a large number of his pictures.

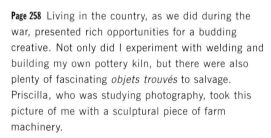

Page 264 Probably because of my early interest in engineering and metalwork, I love images of machinery. This photograph of one of four giant Turbiston bronze propellers being made near London for the German Atlantic liner *Europa* was taken on 1 January 1930; the date probably explains the fellow doffing his hat for the camera.

Page 265 When I had finished the waterfront at Butlers Wharf beside Tower Bridge, it looked simply enormous and I wanted to find some sculptural objects to put on it. I had heard of a scrap yard down at Portsmouth harbour that was filled with nautical scrap, so I took Eduardo Paolozzi, who was no stranger to junk yards, and we bought a big truckload of things, very cheaply, for the cost of the metal alone, most of which was cast iron. This propeller came from there.

Page 266 When we bought the Butlers Wharf complex of warehouses, we found this tiny photograph album of original prints, which had been taken to document the various buildings and the products they stored – tea, ginger, bananas and so forth – as well as the workmen unloading and sorting the cargo. I love these two workshops, especially the carpenter's, where, despite all the mess, you can see his tools neatly lined up and little storage boxes all labelled with their contents.

Page 267 One of my proudest moments came in 1983. We had hired one of those Thames River boats for our design staff Annual Xmas party, and when it got just beyond Tower Bridge, they cut the engines and – with everyone up on deck – I announced that we had just bought the entire complex of derelict wharehouses to develope as flats, offices, shops and restaurants. Just then, a blaze of fireworks shot up from the dark buildings in front of us, that would become known as the Butlers Wharf Project.

Page 268 My son Sebastian is director in charge of product design at my design and architecture company Conran & Partners. He runs a team of 18 designers, as well as doing hands-on design work for a wide range of clients. This can sometimes involve providing inspiration – acting as design mentor, if you like – for the client's own creative team. This project, the technically demanding Koga Spyker racing bike 'Aeroblade', with hand-built aluminium glass fibre-coated carbon composite wheels, was a limited edition of only 50 bikes.

Page 269 My sister Priscilla took this picture of me when she was 17 and studying to be a photographer. During the war, our parents moved to a farmhouse in Liphook, Hampshire, and at the time she was studying at the art school in Guildford, one of the first in the world to teach commercial photography. We both liked this type of farm machinery; I enjoyed its simple, robust, practical design, while she saw its photogenic potential.

Page 270 Some years ago, we were having building work done at Barton Court and one day the electrician arrived with this large heavy object, saying – correctly – that he thought I might like it. Now one of my favourite things, it is a ceramic conductor from some sort of high-voltage power line. The British opera and theatre director Dr Jonathan Miller memorably calls this sort of thing 'the art of the commonplace'.

Page 271 This is a pen-and-ink drawing of the mainspring of a clock by Leonardo da Vinci dating from around 1495. It is one of his many investigations into the workings of things, both mechanical and anatomical. His journals contain drawings for a great many inventions, some of which were workable and greatly ahead of their time, and others that were remarkable flights of fancy. A truly inspirational talent, could he be one of the world's first real product designers?

Page 272 A key part of the design process is creating prototype models. This is my office table at Barton Court, covered with models that were made over the course of about a year. I love them – they are among my greatest pleasures.

Page 273 This is a collage of some of my sketches for new furniture, collected from a number of years' work; the design for the cone chair (fourth row, left) is from the 1950s. My assistant Stuart transfers initial pencil drawings to the computer, gets the proportions right, and then makes a model, which will eventually evolve into a full-size working prototype.

Page 274 This desk was designed by the Italian Carlo Mollino in 1949 for the Casa Orengo. I remember seeing a picture of it in the 1950s in *Domus*, the magazine founded by the inspiring Italian architect and designe, Gio Ponti. I saw the actual desk later at the Milan Trienalle and, to me, it seemed an optimistic and energetic springboard into the future. It perfectly demonstrated the excitement of what I always think of as the Gio Ponti period of Italian design. I know it would inspire me if I sat at it.

Page 275 Over the past few years, I have begun to spend more time in my office at Barton Court rather than in London, but this room above the kitchen has always been a workroom. Ambient light comes from domed recesses, which I made in fibrous plaster and inserted into the false ceiling. I designed the desk, with slide-out extensions, but the chairs around the Castiglioni table are by the Italian architect and designer Mario Bellini. The painting behind the desk is by the British artist Jane Brough.

Page 276 This beautifully laid-out page is from a book that my great-grandfather had. He was a lepidopterist and collected butterflies and moths, which inspired me to do the same. Hawk moths were my real passion – I collected every British type except a 'Deathshead' about 35. What remains of my collection is still stored in an old collector's cabinet in the living room.

Page 277 For my 75th birthday, Priscilla gave me this tiny butterfly collage, which she commissioned from Royal College of Art graduate Sarah Bridgland. Sarah calls her work a celebration of the hybrid: 'As a passionate collector, I combine cut-outs of found and drawn imagery to create intimately scaled three-dimensional collages.'

Page 278 My son Jasper recently refurbished the most beautiful townhouse in Sackville Street, London, and created a showcase for his fashion and home collections, of which this recent edition, made in conjunction with the fine china company Wedgwood, is called 'Blue Butterfly'. I particularly like the way he has reinterpreted a traditional eighteenth-century design in watercolour and scattered the elements randomly across plates, bowls and cups, leaving plenty of white space.

Page 279 Throughout the 1950s, I worked on a freelance basis for Midwinter Potteries, producing a number of designs for its new 'Fashion' ranges. Radical at the time, they featured rimless plates and bowls in nonspherical shapes. One range was decorated with my drawings of vegetables, and another with whimsical depictions of cars, planes, buses and steam engines. This piece, my first, is from the 'Nature Study' range that was launched in 1955. It is my favourite, and still sits on the shelf in my office at Barton Court.

Pages 280–281 When I redid my office a few years ago, I installed these invisibly supported shelves all along one wall. It is a good place to store fragile models of the furniture I have designed, as well as a flexible showcase for anything else that might catch my eye or arrive in the post. The 'Chiavari' chair (see page 161) is one of those I was selling in 1956.

Page 282 Designed by the Canadian architect Wells Coates (see page 27) in 1935, Embassy Court on the seafront in Brighton was the first building in Britain to have penthouse apartments, as well as sundecks and its own restaurant. In 2003 Conran & Partners was called in to lead a team – which included Bluestorm, the company set up by the owner-occupiers – to restore the building after years of neglect. The project took two years to complete and Embassy Court is now once again an exceptional example of modernist design.

Page 283 The smooth, Cubist forms of this Indian pueblo in Taos, New Mexico (photographed by T. Harmon Pankhurst around 1910), developed organically as more additions were made to the village, creating a complex of enclosed courtyards, flat roofs and layered boxes. Built from adobe, a mixture of tightly compacted earth, clay and straw, such buildings are ideal for hot climates as they absorb and release heat slowly. This simple block-like architecture was first used by Native Americans in south-western America and Latin America.

Page 284 I have often said that the Seagram Building on Park Avenue in New York – designed by Ludwig Mies van der Rohe in association with Philip Johnson – is one of my favourite buildings and I still think it takes some beating. This elevation drawing by Johnson emphasizes the satisfying rhythm of the bronze-finished structure, which is expressed in the vertical beams that extend all the way up the vast curtain-wall of glass. Nobody has done it better.

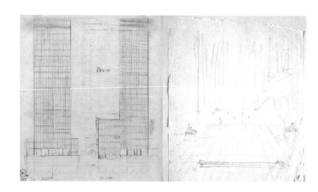

Page 285 The 39-storey Seagram Building was completed in 1958 and was famously set back 27m (90ft) from the building line. This extraordinarily casual 1954 sketch shows Mies van der Rohe considering ideas for planting and statues for the public plaza in front of the entrance.

Page 286 Made from 120 pillars of Guadarrama granite blocks, this aqueduct is a masterpiece of aesthetics and engineering. It was built by the Romans around AD50 to provide water for the Spanish city of Segovia. At its centre the structure is more than 28m (93ft) high, thus necessitating two tiers of arches, but, incredibly, it was constructed without the use of mortar. Despite its designation in 1985 as a World Heritage Site, the aqueduct is currently suffering from a lack of maintenance and is beginning to deteriorate and crack.

Page 287 The Millau Viaduct by Norman Foster and the French structural engineer Michel Virlogeux is a spectacular feat of engineering. Spanning the 3km (2 mile) Tarn Gorge in France at a maximum height of 246m (807ft), it felt like being on the deck of the world's biggest, most elegant liner when I drove across it recently. Foster described the structure as 'a bridge that would march across the valley from one side to the other in the most elegant, economical light, modular fashion. And along the way, there would be an incident that would be a river.'

Page 288 The marvellous Sydney Harbour Bridge is the largest steel-arch bridge in the world. It was designed by the Australian engineer Dr J. C. C. Bradfield, but Ralph Freeman, the consulting engineer for the British construction firm Dorman Long & Co, must also be acknowledged. Begun in 1924, the bridge took 1,400 men eight years to build. In February 1932 the strength of the finished bridge was tested when 96 locomotives were lined up end to end across the main span.

Page 289 I love bridges: the Clifton Suspension Bridge in England, the Golden Gate in California and the Firth of Forth in Scotland, shown here. There is something satisfying about them it is something to do with their symmetry, their completeness and their structural detail. There have been some wonderful modern footbridges built recently, too: Wilkinson Eyre's 'winking' Millennium Bridge at Gateshead in England, Santiago Calatrava's Campo Volantin in Bilbao, Spain, and, of course, Norman Foster's 'wobbly' bridge beside Tate Modern in London.

Page 290 I love the way you can see the structure of timber-framed buildings. When you walk into a medieval tithe barn and look up at the network of timbers, you understand what a remarkable piece of structural engineering it is. This vast barn in Cressing Temple, Essex, was made from 472 oaks felled between 1257 and 1290, and is 40m (130ft) long, 12m (39ft) wide and 11m (36ft) high. I had one almost as good as this at our house in Norfolk, and we used it as a studio to photograph the first Habitat catalogue in 1969.

Page 291 The superb hammer-beam roof of Westminster Hall in London was added to the original eleventh-century building between 1394 and 1401. The roof was designed and built by the master mason Henry Yevele and his master carpenter Hugh Herland. To create this soaring space, the tie beams that support the roof were cut through, leaving shorter hammer beams on either side, which were supported by curved braces.

Page 292 I like the integrated nature of this 1930s shopfront for Cresta Silks in Brighton. Edward McKnight Kauffer, the American artist and designer responsible for all those wonderful posters for London Transport, did the lettering set against a glass backing, which fits perfectly with the Wells Coates façade. Only the rather limp window display lets it down.

Page 293 One of the most exciting projects I ever did was the 21 Shop for Woolands in Knightsbridge, London, around 1960. Not only was the shop a real breakthrough in women's clothing for 21-year-olds, but I still think our design broke new ground in its fascia and interior. I worked on it with a team of Royal College of Art students, as I was teaching at the time. It isn't often I see something I did then in the past and think I couldn't do it better today. The inspiration behind it was the MD of Woolands, Martin Moss; he should get the credit.

Page 294 Layered black walls, black marble floors and a dark ceiling sparkling like the night sky – this is the Collectors' Club, part of the Crystal Worlds Shop that our design studio created in Wattens in Austria for Swarovski. Showcases along the walls and free-standing vitrines display the latest additions to its ranges, and the two binocular-style discs are etched-glass windows. We also put in groups of black leather 'Bibendum' chairs by the modernist designer Eileen Gray.

Pages 296–297 How can you have a book about Inspiration without including the pyramids? I like all pyramids even the glass pyramid by the Chinese-American architect I. M. Pei inside the courtyard of the Paris Louvre takes your breath away when you first see it. This, of course, is the Giza plateau outside Cairo, with the great pyramids of Cheops, Chephren and Mycerinus. I remember the first time I saw them, I was with my first wife, Brenda.

Pages 298–299 This awe-inspiring pen-and-wash drawing from the Bibliothèque Nationale in Paris is the work of the French neoclassical architect Etienne-Louis Boullée. Produced in the 1780s, it is a proposal for a pyramidal cenotaph to commemorate Henri de la Tour d'Auvergne, Vicomte de Turenne. The Vicomte, who died in 1675, had been one of the most highly regarded military commanders in Europe and a Marshal General of France. Napoleon said of him, 'His genius grew bolder as it grew older'.

Pages 300–301 The landscape photographer Murray Fredericks took this photograph among the vivid turquoise glaciers and icebergs in the Errera Channel in Antarctica. I find it a good example of how the earth, seen through the eyes of some brilliant photographers, has a neverending capacity to amaze us.

Page 332 As you may know, I am a passionate pyrotechnic and every ten years since my 50th, I have celebrated my birthdays with spectacular fireworks, initially on the lawns at Barton Court but latterly from a barge moored on the Thames in front of my Butlers Wharf restaurants. The last time I was staying in Sydney in Australia, the firework display from the famous harbour bridge (see page 288) was one of the most magnificent events of my life.

Page 295 I have a lot of memories of Top Shop, as I have of the retail group Next, which we created. One of its first appearances was on the top floor of the Peter Robinson store in Richmond, which the Conran Design Group designed in 1965. Our company brochure from the time explains: 'The client's budget was an important factor in determining the design treatment. As a result we made maximum use of simple, inexpensive materials – rough sawn timber, painted chipboard panelling and sisal carpets.' A far cry from retail budgets today.

Page 333 Painted by Eric Ravilious (see page 78) in 1933 when he was living in Stratford Road in Kensington, this picture, entitled *November 5th* (Guy Fawkes Night, of course), was exhibited in his one-man show in London that same month. Ravilious, like me, was very fond of fireworks; earlier that year he had painted a night-scene mural, with rockets and Roman candles, for the Midland Hotel in Morecambe. At the moment, I am designing a box of fireworks to sell at The Conran Shop for its 21st birthday.

The publisher would like to thank the following contributors for their kind permission to reproduce the following photographs:

1 ©Salvador Dali, Gala-Salvador Dali Foundation, DACS, London 2008; 2-3 Skyscan/Flight Images; 4 Artist: Tom Conran; 5 Kulbir Thandi; 6 David Brittain; 8 Paul Massey/LivingEtc/IPC; 10 David Brittain; 12-13 Jon Chidsey; 14-15 Andrew Lawson/Conran Octopus; 16 David Brittain; 18 Alexandre Bailhache; 19 Ken Kirkwood/Conran Octopus; 20 Alexandre Bailhache; 21 Chris Tubbs/Conran Octopus; 22 David Garcia; 23 Tino Tedaldi; 24 General Photographic Agency/Hulton Archive/Getty Images; 25 NMeM Daily Herald Archive/Science & Society ; 26 Simon Brown; 27 above Collection Centre Canadien d'Architecture/Canadian Centre for Architecture, Montreal; 27 centre General Photographic Agency/Hulton Archive/Getty Images; 27 below David Riley/Alamy; 28 Artist: Michael Wyckham; 30 Snowdon/Camera Press London; 31 Chris Tubbs/Conran Octopus; 32-33 Ken Kirkwood/Conran Octopus; 34 Camera Press/Schoener Wohnen; 35-36 Snowdon/Camera Press London; 37 David Brittain; 38 Chris Tubbs/Conran Octopus; 39 John Maltby/RIBA Library Photographs Collection; 40 Kulbir Thandi; 41 David Garcia; 42 'Head' 1955, Materials Pen and ink on paper, Measurements 35.50 x 28.00 cm, Scottish National Gallery of Modern Art © Trustees of the Paolozzi Foundation, DACS, London 2008; 43 Jill Kennington/Hulton Archive/Getty Images; 44 NASA/JPL/University of Arizona; 45-48 David Brittain; 49 (Constantin Brancusi,1876-1957, Vue d'atelier avec les grand coqs et le Roi des rois (d'apres triage moderne).Musee National d'Art Moderne, Centre Georges Pompidou ©CNAC/MNAM Dist. RMN. All rights reserved. ADAGP, Paris & DACS, London 2008; 50-52 David Brittain; 53 David Garcia; 54-55 Michael Wyckham; 56 Ray Williams; 58 John Maltby/RIBA Library Photographs Collection; 59 Richard Dennis Publications; 60-61 Ray Williams; 62 City of Westminster Archives Centre; 63 Kettles Yard, Cambridge; 64 John Maltby/RIBA Library Photographs Collection; 65 Herman Miller Inc; 66 Vitra Design Museum; 67 The Museum of Modern Art, New York/Scala, Florence ©Mies van der Rohe Archive (Sketch of chairs with split bent-wood frames and steel-rod reinforecement 1934-35, coloured pencil on paper); 68-69 John Maltby/RIBA Library Photographs Collection; 70-71 David Brittain; 72 Image courtesy of the Museum & Contemporary Collection, Central St Martins College of Art & Design; 73 John Maltby/RIBA Library Photographs Collection; 74 Alexandre Bailhache; 75 David Garcia; 76 Central Press/Getty Images; 77 Illustrator: Tony Meeuwissen; 78 Courtesy of Sally Hunter Fine Art ©Estate of Eric Ravilious/DACS, London 2008; 80-81 Snowdon/Camera Press London; 82 Ken Kirkwood/Conran Octopus; 83 Romas Foord; 84-85 Paul Massey/LivingEtc/IPC; 86 Illustrator: Oscar Montelius; 87 Kulbir Thandi; 88-89 David Brittain; 90 Debi Treloar; 91 David Brittain; 92 above Courtesy of Daniel Benard; 92 below Christian Sarramon; 93 Kulbir Thandi; 95 Catherine Gratwicke; 98 Dominic Blackmore; 100-101 Christopher Simon Sykes/The World of Interiors (Raby Castle); 103 Derry Moore; 104 Brent Archive; 105 Jean Cazals; 106 H.H.

Johnston/Royal Geographical Society; 107 Roger-Viollet/Topfoto; 109 Georgia Glynn-Smith/Conran Octopus; 110-111 John Maltby/RIBA Library Photographs Collection; 112 Illustrator: Agneta Neroth; 115 John Thomson/V&A Images/Victoria and Albert Museum; 116-117 David Brittain; 118-119 Robert Doisneau/Rapho/Eyedea; 120 David Garcia; 121 Marc Schwartz (Taken from 'Everyday Things; Kitchen Ceramics' by Suzanne Slesin, Daniel Rosztroch & Stafford Cliff published by Abbeville Press 1997); 122 Artist: Lars Zech; 123 Kulbir Thandi; 125 John Maltby/RIBA Library Photographs Collection; 126 Pete Hill/David Mellor Design; 127 Jeremy Phillips for Fairfax House, York; 128 John Maltby/RIBA Library Photographs Collection; 129 Habitat; 130 David Garcia; 131 RIBA Library Photographs Collection; 133 Gustavsberg; 134 Leeds Library & Information Services; 135 Ben Nicholson ©Angela Verren Taunt 2007, All rights reserved. DACS, London 2008, Courtesy Bernard Jacobsen Gallery; 136 David Garcia; 137 akg-images ©Succession Picasso/DACS, London 2008; 138 David Brittain; 139 Vicki Conran; 140 Christian Sarramon; 141 Artist: William Roberts; 142 Richard Leeney; 143 John Maltby/RIBA Library Photographs Collection; 145 RIBA Library Drawings Collection; 146 David Brittain; 147 Jorge Lewinski © The Lewinski Archive at Chatsworth; 150 Image courtesy of The Potteries Museum & Art Gallery, Stoke-on-Trent; 151 David Brittain; 153 Ditte Isager; 154-155 Architectural Drawings Collection/The Danish National Art Library; 156 John Maltby/RIBA Library Photographs Collection; 157 Robin Hayes Photography; 159 David Brittain; 160 Tim Rieman; 161 Popperfoto/Getty Images; 162 Christopher Simon Sykes/Conde Nast Publications Ltd (Artist: Henry Brudenell-Bruce); 163 Aya Tokunaga/Casa Brutus; 164 Geffrye Museum; 165 Andrew Wittner (Taken from Memories by Graham Cornall); 166 Popperfoto/Getty Images; 168 David Brittain; 169 Private Collection; 170 Snowdon/Camera Press London; 172 RIBA Library Photographs Collection; 173 David Garcia; 174 Courtesy of the Francesca Galloway Gallery; 175 David Brittain (Taken from 'Indian Style' by Suzanne Slesin & Stafford Cliff published by Clarkson N Potter Inc 1990); 178 Chris Tubbs; 179 David Garcia; 180 David Brittain; 181 ©The Trustees of the British Museum; 182 Ken Kirkwood/Conran Octopus; 183 David Brittain; 184-185 Gebruder Thonet Vienna; 186 Henry Bourne(Art director: Sue Skeen); 188 Artist: Ned Conran; 189 Foundation Helene Adant, Bibliotheque Kandinsky, Centre Georges Pompidou; 190 'Water Pouring into Swimming Pool, Santa Monica' 1964, Lithograph in four colours, 19x25"(c)David Hockney; 192 Ken Kirkwood/Conran Octopus; 193 Snowdon/Camera Press London; 194-197 David Garcia; 198-200 Chris Tubbs/Conran Octopus; 201 Boyer/Roger-Viollet/Getty Images; 204 ©Christie's Images Ltd., 1994; 206 Austrian Museum of Applied Arts/Contemporary Art ©MAK; 207 David Brittain; 208 Max McMurdo; 209 The World of Interiors; 210 Vicki Conran; 212 M.McNeill/Hulton Archive/Getty Images; 213 Yale Centre for British Art/Paul Mellon Collection USA/Bridgeman Art Library; 214 above Jon Chidsey; 214 below & 215 Stuart Westwell; 216-217 Norman Smith/Hulton Archive/Getty Images; 220 Kunsthistorisches Museum, Vienna/Bridgeman Art Library; 221 Don

McCullin/Axiom; 222 Beans Stamp Pane ©2006 United States Postal Service, All rights reserved. Used with permission; 223 Artist: Rachel Pedder-Smith. Reproduced with the permission of the Director and The Board of Trustees of The Royal Botanic Gardens, Kew, Surrey; 224 Reg Speller/Hulton Archive/Getty Images; 225 Vicki Conran; 227 Gilles de Chabeneix; 228-229 Jacques Dirand/The Interior Archive (Artist: Henry Moore); 230 David Brittain; 231 Royal Horticultural Society; 233 Nancy Sirkis; 234 Chris Eckersley; 235 The National Archives (ref RAIL1149/9 p68); 236 David Brittain; 237 Howard Sooley; 238 Phillips, The International Fine Art Auctioneers UK/ Photo © Bonhams, London/Bridgeman Art Library; 239 Howard Sooley; 240 John Amand; 241 Ingo Maurer GmbH; 242 Hunterian Museum & Art Gallery, University of Glasgow; 243 Museen der Stadt Vienna; 244 Romas Foord (2004); 245 British Council ©Estate of Eric Ravilious/DACS, London 2008; 246 David Brittain; 247 Ken Kirkwood (Taken from 'Living Under Glass' published by Clarkson N Potter Inc 1986); 248 Estate of Buckminster Fuller; 249 Edmund Sumner/View; 250 Kim Taylor/DK Limited/Corbis; 252 Marc Schwartz; 253 Kulbir Thandi; 255 Michelin Tyre Public Limited Company; 257 Tino Tedaldi; 258 Priscilla Carluccio; 259 David Brittain; 260 Robeya Photography; 262 David Brittain; 263 Aberdeen Art Gallery & Museums Collections; 264 Fox Photos/Hulton Archive/Getty Images; 265 David Brittain; 269 Priscilla Carluccio; 270 David Brittain; 271 akg-images/ Electa; 272 Alexandre Bailhache; 274 Museo Casa Mollino, Torino; 275 David Garcia; 277 David Brittain (Artist:www.sarahbridgland.co.uk); 278 Tessa Traeger; 279-281 David Brittain; 282 Collection Centre Canadien d'Architecture/Canadian Centre for Architecture, Montreal; 283 Palace of the Governors (MNM/DCA ref 12463) The New Mexico History Museum; 284 (2008 Digital Image, Seagram Building, Plaza Perspective, New York c1954-58, Pencil on note paper, 22.9x29.8cm Acc:MI5411.2, New York) Mies van der Rohe/Gift of the Architect/MOMA, New York/Scala, Florence; 285 (2007 Digital Image) Mies van der Rohe/Gift of the Architect/MOMA, New York/Scala, Florence; 286 Underwood & Underwood/Corbis; 287 Guichaoua/Alamy; 288 Art Gallery of New South Wales, Australia (Sydney Bridge c1934, Gelatin silver photograph, 29.7x21.5cm. Gift of the Cazneaux family 1975); 289 Imagno/Hulton Archive/Getty Images; 290 Essex County Council; 291 Herbert Felton/Hulton Archive/Getty Images; 292 Architectural Press Archive/RIBA Library Photographs Collection; 293 John Maltby/RIBA Library Photographs Collection; 294 Conran & Partners; 295 John Maltby/RIBA Library Photographs Collection; 296-297 akg-images; 298-299 Bibliotheque Nationale de France; 300-301 Murray L Fredericks; 332 Tim Graham/Getty Images; 333 Private Collection ©Estate of Eric Ravilious/DACS, London 2008

Every effort has been made to trace the copyright holders and we apologize in advance for any unintentional errors or omissions, and would be pleased to insert the appropriate acknowledgment in any subsequent publication.

This book is the work of a very small number of people over a very long time. I am indebted to the photographers who have photographed Terence and his remarkable homes down the years. They would say that it was an easy and pleasurable task, but given Terence's critical and exacting eye, it was also something of a daunting responsibility. To capture the quality of light, the proportions of the spaces, and the relationship of the objects to their surroundings – and still make the rooms LOOK as simple, elegant, and timeless as Terence makes them FEEL. As someone once said to me – it's not only the objects in a room, but the spaces between them, that creates the impact. I am grateful to Terence for giving me the almost impossible opportunity to try and pin down creativity, and what it has meant in his life and throughout his life.

Thank you also, to three very talented people who have helped me in this task. Anne-Marie Hoines, who spent many months tracking down the pictures I needed; Bridget Hopkinson, who has added to and polished our words, and Ian Hammond, who patiently composed it all into the book you now hold in your hands.

In addition, my thanks for the help I received from the following: Denny Andrews, Sandrene Maury Besson, Sarah Bridgland. David Brittain, David Burke, Susan Campbell, Priscilla Carluccio, Jonathan Chidsey, Jasper Conran, Ned Conran, Sebastian Conran, Sophie Conran, Tom Conran, Vicki Conran, Jane Creech, Polly Dickens, Chris Eckersley, Kim Edwards, Maggie Heaney, Nu-Nu Yee Hoggarth, Emilie Lemons, Max McMurdo, Karin Murray, Peter Prescott, Mat Riches, Daniel Rozensztroch, Marc Schwartz, John Scott, Shiri Slavin, Suzy Slesin, Kulbir Thandi, Debbie Treloar, Brian and Gail Webb, Stuart Westwell, Laura Whitton, Ray Williams and Patricia Woods.

Finally, my thanks to the Conran Octopus team, whose enthusiasm and support drove the project forward, and to Conran & Partners, The Conran Shop, Conran Ink and Benchmark teams, who contributed so much, so enthusiastically.
Stafford Cliff, 2008

I'd need this entire book to list the literally thousands of people that I have worked with over the years, including this book's author, the creative Stafford Cliff. Top of the list must be my mother, Christina, who devoted herself to seeing that my sister Priscilla, and I received the best creative education possible during those straightened war years. She put books and art exhibitions in front of us and literally sold the family silver to pay for our design education. Thanks for your genes mother.

At Bryanston school I was enormously influenced in the arts and crafts by Don Potter (a pupil of Eric Gill) and by Charles Handley Reed who made the History of Design fascinating.

At the Central school Eduardo Paolozzi and his work became my greatest influence which has continued over the years, while Miss Dora Batty, who ran the textile course, opened my eyes to historical textiles.

In the real world I met Michael Wickham, a Condé Nast photographer and man of a multitude of talents including making things, but it was his style of life that I found most influential. He took me on my first trip to France. He liked food, too and cooked very well. He was a Bordeaux communist.

Oliver Gregory was probably the most inspiring design director I worked with. He was intensely practical, having trained as a shopfitter, and an ace at making things happen. He shared my enthusiasm for food, wine and cigars.

Stephen Bayley has an encyclopaedic knowledge of design and is inspirational in his enthusiasm; good (at times) to work with.

John Stephenson, who ran our design group was a constant source of knowledge and technical knowledge, as was Fred Roche and Stuart Moscrop who helped build our architectural practice.

My children, Sebastian, Jasper, Tom, Sophie and Ned have all been interested and critical observers of my creative progress, as have my various wives, particularly Caroline and my current wife Vicki. Shirley helped in the early days of Conran Fabrics; I don't think I would have succeeded without them.

The many artists who were our friends and visitors at Barton Court were all influential, interested and informed about design. Francis Bacon had been an interior decorator; Howard Hodgkin collected modernist furniture and was extremely knowledgeable, as was Richard Smith and David Hockney. Denis Wirth Miller was always full of charming ideas. Their talent and enthusiasm rubbed off and enlarged my horizons. Today I work with Sean Sutcliffe whose practical wood working knowledge is a constant source of inspiration.

Of course there are many contemporary influences – the work of Norman Foster, David Chipperfield and in particular, the amazing Eames office are a constant source of inspiration. But I constantly turn back to Paolozzi's work and the innovation of Victorian engineers.

On the food side I would still be eating spam fritters if Elizabeth David had not had such an astounding influence on creative young people in the '50s. She really did cause a food revolution. Certainly Caroline and Vicki's home cooking and writing have been very influential, as has Simon Hopkinson – a friend and our first chef at Bibendum. Michel Guerard has always seemed to me the most influential French chef with a robust view of food that I admire. As had my friend the wine merchant and bon viveur Bill Baker who was a great influence on my enjoyment of eating and drinking. Finally, a few of my current inspirational collaborators: Diarmuid Gavin, Peter Prescott, Jonathan Christie, Karin Murray, Jill Webb, Stuart Westwell, Jeremy Lee, Priscilla Carluccio, the team at C&P and of course, Vicki C. *Terence Conran, 2008*

First published in 2008
by Conran Octopus Limited,
a part of Octopus Publishing Group,
2–4 Heron Quays, London E14 4JP
www.octopusbooks.co.uk

A Hachette Livre UK Company
www.hachettelivre.co.uk

Book Concept & Design: Stafford Cliff
Publisher: Lorraine Dickey
Managing Editor: Sybella Marlow
Copy Editor: Bridget Hopkinson
Art Director: Jonathan Christie
Production Artwork: Ian Hammond
Picture Researcher: Anne-Marie Hoines
Production Manager: Katherine Hockley

ISBN: 978 1 84091 494 8
Printed in Hong Kong

Cover blocking: This prophetic symbol comes from the cover of a book entitled *The Practice of Design*, which was given to me as the old boys prize when I left Bryanston school in the summer of 1948, to take up a place at the Central School of Arts and Crafts. In part of his introduction to the book, Herbert Read said: 'But let us keep the distinction clear between what we find and what we invent: between what we take from nature and admire and imitate, and what we put into nature, above nature, against nature, by virtue of our intellect and intuition. The person – the living and breathing sensibility of the individual – unites everything; but there is all the difference in the world between what goes out from the person, as his signature, and what comes into the person, as the inexorable law of his environment, or as the voice of God'.

Endpapers: Aspects of design, taken from an early edition of *Larousse Universel*, 1922.

Page 1: One of Salvador Dalí's studies for the dream sequence in Hitchcock's *Spellbound*, 1945.

Page 2–3: Aerial view of Barton Court.

Page 335: One of the sauce boats I designed for Royal Doulton.

DESSIN LINEAIRE

Règle

Double décimètre

Té

Pistolet

Equerre

Rapporteur

FIGURES GÉOMÉTRIQUES

Crayon

Plume

Tire-ligne

Pinceau

Gomme

Solitaire

Godet

Compas

DESSINS GÉOMÉTRIQUES

TEINTE ET OMBRE AU LAVIS

DESSIN COTÉ

350 mm

Fil à plomb

Portecrayon

Estompes

Mannequin

DESSIN DE MÉCANIQUE

Plan

DESSIN D'ARCHITECTURE

Élévation

Coupe

DESSIN AU TRAIT

DESSIN D'ORNEMENT

Album

M. DESSERTENNE

CROQUIS D'APRÈS NATURE

Paul Renouard

PAYSAGE MIS EN PERSPECTIVE